A MIRACLE EVERY DAY

ALSO BY MARITA GOLDEN

Wild Women Don't Wear No Blues

And Do Remember Me

Long Distance Life

A Woman's Place

Migrations of the Heart

Saving Our Sons

Skin Deep

The Edge of Heaven

A Miracle Every Day

TRIUMPH AND TRANSFORMATION IN THE LIVES OF SINGLE MOTHERS

MARITA GOLDEN

ANCHOR BOOKS
DOUBLEDAY
New York
London
Toronto
Sydney
Auckland

AN ANCHOR BOOK

PUBLISHED BY DOUBLEDAY

a division of Random House, Inc.

1540 Broadway, New York, New York 10036

ANCHOR BOOKS, DOUBLEDAY, and the portrayal of
an anchor are trademarks of Doubleday, a division of
Random House, Inc.

Book design by Julie Duquet

From "A Creation Story," © Janet Maloney Franze, which
appears in CHILD OF MINE, edited and © copyright 1997 by
Christina Baker Kline. Reprinted with permission by Hyperion.

Library of Congress Cataloging-in-Publication Data
Golden, Marita.
  A miracle every day: triumph and transformation in the
lives of single mothers / by Marita Golden. — 1st ed.
      p.   cm.
    1. Single mothers.   2. Single-parent family.   3. Children
of single parents.   I. Title.
  HQ759.915.G63   1999
  306.874'3—dc21   98-30942
                                                    CIP

ISBN 0-385-48315-5

10   9   8   7   6   5   4   3   2   1

For Michael

A MIRACLE EVERY DAY

I always wanted to be a mother. To one child. And I was not afraid to raise that child alone. I planned to be a mother one day, even at the age of twenty-two, while living in New York City and studying at the Graduate School of Journalism at Columbia University and daily discovering and reconfiguring my ambition. I would be a mother, even if I had to do it alone.

This yearning was intertwined, quite compatibly and quite logically, it seemed to me, with the determination to write and to explore and claim as much of the world as I could. And through some act monumental or minuscule, I would, as well, contribute to the progress of my people, and maybe even of the world. Race-woman with a baby at her breast, the fingers of her free hand resting on the typewriter keys. The image filled me not with fear but with greedy anticipation. I secretly knew, even then, that to have a child was a profoundly important act of narration. Yet I never felt that the story I would write as "mother" would subvert the articles I was writing then and the books that lay in wait.

A child is a chronicle. As in any saga, the one composed by mother and child revises assumptions and unsettles the too-neat line of demarcation we often draw between what is possible and what is real. Motherhood offered me another way into the world, even as it demanded and required everything and then forced me, like a weary scavenger, to search for still more. Honor thy mother, thy father, thy child.

My own mother was unprepared and, she once confessed to me, absolutely amazed when she became pregnant with me at forty-two. It was in the summer of my nineteenth year that my mother told me she had never thought of aborting me, although her relationship with my father was turbulent and I was an unplanned child. This secret history spilled forth in the aftermath of my revelation that I feared I was pregnant and was thinking of having an abortion. As a counternarrative, my mother told me that I was a child who became, once my existence was confirmed, retroactively longed-for and totally desired. The year of my birth, my mother owned several boarding houses, played and often won at the numbers, drove her own Pontiac, and frequently hosted parties that featured marathon games of poker and

bid whist on the first floor, and games of craps in the basement of the houses she owned.

As we sat on my mother's chenille-covered four-poster
the day I spoke of a pregnancy I feared, and my mother of a
pregnancy she embraced, she recalled, nonetheless, with
chagrin and a pain she could not camouflage, how her
friends teased her about her middle-aged pregnancy. Years
later, after I had become a mother, I searched through all
the black and white photos of my family in vain for a
picture of my mother pregnant. There were cracked and
aged pictures of my mother lying on a blanket on the sand
of some segregated beach with friends, or standing before
her mother's modest house on McConnell Road in Greens-
boro, North Carolina, in the summer when she came to
take me home to Washington after I'd spent six weeks with
Granny Reid. And there was the three-by-five black and
white photo of her guiding my five-year-old hand in the
cutting of a cake at my first big birthday party, a picture I
always searched for first each time I opened the album. But
there were no photos of my mother, a large woman, made
larger still because her body was filled with me.

Those nine months were not (as far as I know) captured
on film and, by the snapping of the lens, honored, legiti-
mized, saved. The body of a pregnant woman is lauded as a
temple in cultural mythology, yet evokes the oddest, most
intense mixture of obsession and revulsion. The body sup-
posedly held sacred is vulnerable to blatant assessment and
even mockery. The body of a woman "with child" some-

times seems to belong to everyone in the world, really, but her. When I failed to find any photos of my mother pregnant, I searched through my own photo album and found none of me carrying my son. Is this erasure, or willful amnesia, or a conspiracy to somehow obliterate the act that perhaps more than any other defines the lives of so many women, women like my mother, women like me? The stiff pages of the photo album I kept in honor of the family my husband and I had created held scores of christening pictures, dozens of photos that captured every moment of my son's growth; but the bulky, weighty, "foreign" body that had been the site of the most astonishing incubation was nowhere framed or frozen in time by either me or my mother.

I did not want the child I feared I carried at nineteen. I was still in college and had cast myself, and been cast by the cultural eruptions of that time, as an unalterably modern woman. Controlling my fate was everything to me. I was young, filled with the hubris and vanity of the young, and thought controlling my destiny was purely a matter of determination. I wanted a child when I could make promises to that child, and to myself, that I was sure I could keep.

If I had an abortion it would not have been an illegal, possibly lethal operation, the kind my mother had described to me as common for many of the women of her generation. I could walk openly into a legal clinic. I could safely and freely make an appointment for a qualified doctor to abort my child. My mother argued against the abortion I was considering, if I was indeed pregnant. In fact, my period was horribly, uncharacteristically late, but I was not pregnant. My mother's relationship with my father often sapped much of what was strong and pure and beautiful in her. Still, as she later recalled, when she knew that she was pregnant, "It never occurred to me to have an abortion because I thought if I did, I'd be denying the world someone who might do great things. What if I killed a scientist, a doctor, someone who could make the world a better place?" My mother asked this question rhetorically, but with an arc of emotion that in its strength echoed the feelings of nearly twenty years earlier. "I would never forgive myself," she concluded.

Some may hear in those words an elitist valuation of human life. What if my mother had aborted a being who grew into a man or woman known only for the unremarkable nature of their life, someone who steadfastly shunned the extraordinary? Wasn't that a life worth saving too? But what I hear in my mother's plea are the awesome expectations she possessed. She was a black woman in 1950, carrying a child for whom she could predict and assert only the ability to amaze, to act upon and in the world in powerful, positive ways.

I can imagine how awkward my mother must have felt wearing maternity clothes, how morning sickness must have struck her as a cruel, twisted joke at forty-two, when, as she told me, "I thought I had gone through the change of life. I didn't even know I could still get pregnant." Even her language is revealing, the way she spoke of "the change of life" rather than menopause, moving from fertility to infertility, growing out of youth and into age. Even as chagrin and embarrassment competed with wonder, my mother imposed upon me—foetal, existent though only partially formed—the grandest of expectations. Maybe I wasn't a full person yet. But she must've felt the presence of my soul as well as my heartbeat.

In her decision to give me life, my mother christened and launched herself. I assume she felt that I would be some kind of miracle poised against the heartache of her tumultuous and sometimes violent relationship with my father. The odds might have been stacked against my birth as the inspiration for the kind of love she hoped for, but never knew, with my father; but my mother said yes to me to see what would happen. A talented, skilled gambler, she convinced herself that those nine months were a bet she could win. My mother was brave enough to have left the South; thousands of dollars had been placed in her large eager palms by numbers backers; she regularly came to the rescue of friends and family with succor and financial assistance; she was a mini-legend among her friends; and she loved and had married my father, a man who considered himself the eighth wonder of the world. My mother must've felt that I was a sign, a portent, a charm. Clearly her luck hadn't run out yet.

It ran out when she left my father and became a single mother at fifty-five. But I saw my father every week. My mother had walked out of his life. He refused to leave ours.

When I vowed to become a mother and to parent a child

"by any means necessary," as it were, the ease with which I imagined myself with child and without a husband was rooted, I am sure, in the lives of the many women surrounding me as I grew up.

My two most cherished childhood and adolescent friends were raised by single mothers, as was the cousin to whom I am closest. In the boarding house in which we lived before my parents separated, my best friend among the roomers was a young nurse raising her two-year-old son, Tommy, in a single room on the second floor, a room furnished with a bed, a crib, a chest of drawers, and a record player.

I grew up surrounded, it seemed, by female invincibility, by women who were workers and mothers and sisters and friends and the children of their own mothers. These were women who belonged, I always felt, to the children they raised, the supervisors who paid them, the pastors they praised on Sunday morning. Somehow I could not imagine them belonging entirely to themselves. Courage was the password in countless small dramas staged impromptu in the grocery store, negotiations with the landlord, the phone company, conferences with teachers, expeditions to buy school clothes, wiping up a fevered child's sickness from the bathroom floor. I never thought these women ached with weariness in the darkness at night; or mastered the art of weeping completely yet silently, so no one could hear; or chiseled deserved anger into a stark object of beauty so perfect they were afraid to even touch it.

The battlefields were domestic. The rate of attrition high.

Few medals were given. After all, they were merely mothers. Valor was assumed. Every family has some ancestral lore woven into its bloodstream that would tell, if anyone asked, of some female cousin or aunt or sister who couldn't or wouldn't give in to motherhood, who lit out for the city, the North, or some territory inside herself, and left the children behind. Then there were the few "chosen" women, beautiful or smart or both, who had had "accidental" children gently pulled from their breast so as not to encumber their march toward a place in some Negro college or a job with "the government" or the yearning to make it as a singer, a dancer, anything that would save them from a colored woman's fate, or a single mother's destiny.

But those women are spoken of in whispers, if at all. There are sporadic, partial requiems for the children left behind. It is the mothers—single, singular, solitary—who formed, as it were, an army we never had to acknowledge because everyone knew they would always be there. I felt no fear at the prospect of raising a child alone, for I was once a little black girl imbibing the dogma of independence and forewarned of the world's dangers, embedded in my mother's teachings and in her touch. She would have been derelict to have transmitted any other lesson to me.

Many of my childhood friends were raised by single mothers, who appeared to me as tight-lipped stoics, graceful and long-suffering. Only when those friends and I grew into young women did the secrets tumble forth, in tales of mothers who raged openly and often about what mother-hood had denied them, who chose never to look back, held their progeny too close, protected too much, never spoke of or forgave absent fathers, took too many lovers or none at all.

With no children of their own to fail, these mothers' daughters sometimes concluded that a terrible wrong had been done. Their childhoods had been warped, corrupted—unintentionally perhaps, but the damage had been done. Still, the mothers had remained, steadfast, flawed, and human.

These women, the mothers of my friends, were neither Sapphire nor Sojourner. In the end maybe they were both, hands on hips, berating the forces that would deny them, righteous warriors capable of all and anything for their children. Like me, they were spiritual daughters, too, of slave mothers, America's original "single mothers," and of every mammy bound by the love of her own child, burdened by the affection and power of another's. I saw all that, and wanted to be a mother still.

Did I long for motherhood because of genes pro-grammed to save the species, the undeniable call of the womb, a conspiracy of culture and conditioning and every doll my mother ever bought me?

Yet many of my girlfriends spoke openly of not wanting children. They did not shun the heresy, were not afraid of blasphemy. I admired those girls for their renegade spunk and daring. They knew who they longed to be instead of Mother, had chosen already their own name. But for me a child would complete my name, not censor or inhibit it.

Motherhood cleansed and baptized me like some necessary massive tidal wave I hungered to meet and to know; it sharpened my sense of myself, and of all the women residing within me. None of the men I've loved, the countries I've lived in or journeyed to, the books I've written, transformed me as did loving and raising my child for a decade as a single parent. The years that I was mother/father/sister/brother/everybody/everything to my son were a crucible and a gift. I raised my child and parented myself as well. We grew up together in startling, never-to-be-forgotten ways. Each attempt to shape a healthy childhood for my son altered who I was and would be as mother, as woman, as person. Learning to love my son unconditionally, I embraced myself wholeheartedly. The ongoing process of teaching my son, Michael, to love himself, and others, with respect and charity, opened my own bruised heart to the love of men.

I divorced my son's father a year after my son was born. I remarried when my son was twelve. The years between that divorce and remarriage bound us and shaped us into an entity that sociologists and bureaucrats and cultural critics thought they knew. But we resisted those definitions and became something singular yet collective, whole, and linked to others in ways that allowed us to make a miracle every day. As an African American single mother, my poster girl was not Murphy Brown, educated, affluent, in control, challenges and obstacles overcome in thirty minutes. My symbol was a second-generation teenaged mother portrayed as single-handedly draining the National Treasury because she was on welfare. Of course, Murphy Brown was a fantasy even for most *white* single mothers; and the young sister was a corruption and a lie.

I mothered and fathered my son during our sojourn together, and in amazing synergistic ways, my son made me. He made me brave, and smart and wise, and creative and cunning. Being a single parent is a job, a calling, an avocation. It is impossible, yet millions of women master its intricacies, and turn it into an expression of genius. It is rewarding, and it is at its essence as much about your soul and your spirit as it is about your child.

Several years ago, I was invited to lecture at a large Midwestern university by a female professor of African American literature. During the long drive from the airport, and in subsequent conversations as the professor, Andrea, shuttled me around the sprawling university during my two-day visit, we talked about our lives. She was an articulate, attractive young woman, made more endearing by her passion and enthusiasm for teaching and literature.

The evening of my departure, as we drove to the airport through several inches of snow, Andrea announced, "By next week, I'll be a mother." She was awaiting finalization of her recent adoption of a three-month-old baby girl. "I thought I'd be married by now," she explained. "But I've been looking. I've been waiting. I've been praying. I don't know when or if it'll happen." With a sweep of her hand toward the wide expanse of now-dormant corn and wheat fields for which the state was famed, she said, "There aren't any black men out here. I got tired of waiting. I wanted someone to love."

Then Andrea giddily told me about the girlfriends who had volunteered to be godmothers and aunts, the baby shower her friends had thrown for her, and the African-inspired christening she planned. When we arrived at the airport, we took leave like old friends, hugging one another and wishing each other well.

As I sat on the plane, returning to Washington and my own son—the someone I loved as much as Andrea already loved the daughter she was adopting—I thought of how incredible and transformative was the journey that Andrea had embarked upon. Even armed with her intelligence, her confidence, and her courage, Andrea could not have suspected how shattering and how redemptive raising her child as a single parent would ultimately be. She would be remade every day, and she would be shaken to the nub and the heart and soul of herself as a woman.

Absolutely everything in her life would change. The single-parent experience is a life, not a lifestyle, one that possesses more gifts than burdens, more opportunities than sacrifices. For the woman with the capacity to live in permanent evolution, who approaches motherhood and parenthood with imagination and bravery and compassion, single parenthood can save and expand her life. Nobody will tell you that, unless they have been there—where yes, the nights are long and the days are too, and success is measured in the incremental, nonstop development of two human beings, both mother and child. Family therapist Audrey Chapman calls single mothers "people makers," referring to the ways in which they create and shape their children's lives. But single mothers are also creating and making themselves. The shaping of a whole, powerful, mother/woman self—that is the real challenge of single motherhood, and the implicit reward. Paying the bills, finding day care, a good school, clothing, feeding a child; these tasks are peripheral to the real challenge for single mothers—creating a healthy whole self out of which you can love and "grow" your child.

THE CHALLENGES ARE real, inescapable, hard to deny. Male children raised in single-parent homes are statistically shown to perform less well in school and have more trouble with the law; girls raised in single-parent homes more frequently get pregnant in their teens and often have problems bonding emotionally with men. These statistics are race-neutral and are advanced as a defining commentary on the lives of all female-headed families. But where are the studies that analyze single-parent families for the strengths of the mothers, the positive coping and adaptive skills learned by the children, the support systems that help make these families "work"? Until complementary data exists that attempts to scientifically find and explain single-parent success—with the same diligence applied to stereotyping through analysis of "failure"—any conversation about the effect of single-parent families on children or mothers is incomplete and suspect.

No one can deny that poverty is greater among single-parent families, that the material, physical, sociological, and psychological stresses on single-parent families are significant. But for all the women I know who have been remade and transformed by their lives as female heads of families, these statistics simply did not matter; for they were too busy loving themselves and their children, and thereby making themselves the exception to what is supposed to be the rule. When I was a single mother I decided that the conventional wisdom was irrelevant to my life and my son. We were not a statistic. We were a family.

During my son's teenaged years, I experienced the kind of moment that is impossible to plan or predict, and which informed me that I had accomplished much of what I had hoped to while raising my son as a single parent.

One January weekend, six months before Michael's graduation from his Pennsylvania boarding school, Westtown, I traveled to New York to publicize the paperback edition of one of my books. My husband, Joe, had planned to take the train up from D.C. on Friday, and Michael would also join us, as he had a long weekend break from Westtown. Joe came down with the flu and stayed home. The Friday morning that Michael arrived, after he got settled in the hotel, we walked around Broadway and had lunch at the Motown Cafe, where while singers impersonated the Temptations and the Supremes, Michael shared his exploits on the basketball team and spoke of already missing Westtown and the friends he had made and would soon leave behind when he graduated in June. After lunch we went to see *Waiting to Exhale* and, walking back to the hotel, talked about men and women and love and choices.

That night the first game between the Chicago Bulls and the Los Angeles Lakers, retooled with a returned Magic Johnson, was scheduled to air at 10 P.M. While waiting for the game to start, we watched the movie *To Wong Foo, Thanks for Everything, Julie Newmar.* The tame, lifeless comedy starred Wesley Snipes and Patrick Swayze as two of three transvestites on an elaborate road trip through the South.

At one point I sighed in frustration at the predictability of the plot. Michael, his six feet two inches sprawled across the other bed in the room, agreed and then said, "But look at them, Mom, they're dressed up like women, so they can show their emotions. They're walking around in high heels and they can cry."

I instinctively lowered the volume and turned to look at my son. At seventeen, he was lanky, baby-faced, yet trying hard to grow a mustache. I looked at his face and saw gazing back at me his father and myself. I had bought him dolls along with trucks and video games, all to try to foster his feminine side. As Michael moved into adolescence, I had initiated and maintained a consistent dialogue with him, sometimes a monologue, about the sexism in rap music, the objectification of women in MTV and BET videos, the need to respect women and to embrace his own feelings of vulnerability, fragility, and fear. While I was a single parent we had been through counseling together, and whenever a crisis loomed on the horizon of his life, I urged Michael to open up, not to shut down; to cry or talk through his anger rather than to ram his fist through a wall.

My son's totally unexpected yet passionately felt observation informed me that he had been listening. Now it was my turn to hear him. Michael confided how, as he watched the film, he felt a perverse envy for the freedom of the three men. "On the basketball court, if I get injured I can't cry if I'm in pain. The other guys would razz me about it. But if a girl trips up the stairs she can bawl like a baby," he declared with a vehemence that startled me. "If a girl breaks off with me and I'm hurt, I can't admit that to my buddies. I have to lie. And you know, Mom, sometimes when I'm with them I lie so much that I begin to believe I wasn't hurt too."

The outrage and the visceral sense of inequity Michael obviously felt at the socialization he had to endure, despite my best efforts, heartened me. For it revealed that, while perhaps at that moment in his life he was not able to permit himself to weep in the presence of his friends, or to honestly reveal his feelings to his buddies, he could at least critique the false, dangerous values of masculinity that trapped him and so many other males. He had at least formulated a language to name the problem, even though he could not yet solve it. That moment was an instant of epiphany for me. For it confirmed that the struggle I had waged to influence a portion of my son's soul had not been in vain.

I shared my own anxieties around gender issues, told Michael that women paid a high price for being female, and that it cost men even more to be male. But I also told him how a few weeks earlier, Joe had come home from the high school where he teaches and informed me that one of his former students had been shot and killed. Joe wept freely and at length as he remembered the young man. I told Michael of Joe's male friends and how they all shared moments of crisis and defeat with one another, and were as honest and intimate and lovingly supportive as any women could be.

We watched the Bulls–Lakers game when it came on. But to me it hardly mattered. I had scored the points I needed. During the years when I was raising Michael alone, talking to him endlessly about women, about men, even as I struggled to sort out the meaning of love and life for myself, my son was listening. With no husband beside me, with fingers crossed, propelled mostly by faith, I believed that I could raise a son who would want to honor what was feminine in him as well as that which was masculine, and who would someday learn that all of it belonged to him. I laid the foundation for who I wanted my son to become—a sensitive, thoughtful, perceptive young man who would not take the world at face value. This is what he became.

For all the warnings that the odds are against you, the most critical enemy faced by a woman who is a female head of family (the term I prefer) is doubt. The doubt is in many ways justified when the immensity of the task is considered, but it need not be paralyzing or persistent. We shepherd our children through their lives with the aid and the love of family; of friends and neighbors; and of institutions ranging from school to church. Are you truly a single mother, or are you a woman working in tandem with a community and a world full of personal and material and institutional resources to help you "grow" a healthy child?

The inner journey, however, which so powerfully defines the meaning of single motherhood, is the adventure that we feel least equipped to initiate. Many single mothers who work energetically and quite successfully to provide materially for their children, neglect their own emotional wounds, inflicting them on their children like a dreaded inheritance. Above all, a single-parent home requires a mother/parent intent on opening herself and her child to the qualities of compassion, love, and respect for themselves individually and as a family unit. The single mother must develop the ability in herself and in her child to extend those qualities to others. These are the tools both mother and child require, like psychological oxygen, in order to avoid the traps of self-pity, anger, bitterness, or a sense of betrayal—emotions that fester beneath the calm exterior that many single mothers and their children present to the world.

Every child wants a father they can know, can bond with, and who is always near. Many women feel that a happy marriage is their due. Navigating the treacherous path through the lives we have received, as opposed to the ones we planned, is the test for everyone. It is a challenge especially difficult for single mothers, because so often they feel that they must do it alone.

But developing an inner emotional life as a single parent is the first step in helping your child to do the same. Learning to be reflective and self-critical, to assess one's own choices and actions as objectively as we would judge a stranger's, and in the process to extend charity and understanding to oneself and others, is an evolution that is life-long. It is a way of living one's life, and it is the most important thing our children can see us do. It is a skill that single mothers need in abundance in order to avoid making martyrs of themselves and demons of absent fathers. We need to chisel a safe space in the hearts of our children where they can feel and explore and shape the myriad complex and contradictory emotions they feel about themselves and their lives in single-parent homes. Help them realize that they carry a safe place within them, in their own hearts and minds.

The stories that follow celebrate the resilience of women who are single mothers, women whose greatest strength is their ability to allow their children to re-create them; whose genius lies in their willingness to recognize the interdependence of self-love and maternal love; whose wisdom is in their recognition that mother is one of the most awesome and generous and life-giving designations they could ever have.

A MOTHER'S LOVE

"I had to do everything and it just made me stronger."

M y mother infused in me an indefatigable desire to succeed. She told me that I was the best, despite what the conditions around me suggested. I had been made by God and God didn't make junk." This vigorous affirmation of a single parent's love and influence was made by Michael Lindsey, a graduate of Howard University's School of Social Work who has turned his background as the child of a single mother into a lens to shape his perspective as a social science researcher. Lindsey's master's thesis at Howard was a study entitled, "Resilient Characteristics of African American Males from Single Parent Homes."

Raised with his four brothers by his mother, Charlotte

Carter, in Southeast Washington, Lindsey was deeply invested emotionally in the study, which was funded by a fellowship from the School of Social Work underwritten by Bill and Camille Cosby.

Explaining the motivation for his research, Lindsey states in the introduction to the study that "the situation of African American males from father-absent homes is often examined from a pathological perspective. Attention to those individuals who succeed in such situations has been almost nonexistent in social science literature." The results of Michael Lindsey's study seem to codify what many in the African American community have long known. I found the fact that research was being conducted to validate this knowledge exciting and momentous in its import. In his study of twenty black males living in Washington, D.C., between the ages of eighteen and thirty-four from various backgrounds, Lindsey sought to find the "resilient characteristics" nurtured in the men by their single-parent mothers—the characteristics that had enabled them to grow into mature men and productive citizens.

The factors that had most indelibly shaped the men were: strong external support from the community; the ability to find meaning in personal suffering; racial consciousness; valuing family; recognizing the importance of spirituality; involvement in sports; being willing to challenge competitors; having open communication with the mother; possessing multidimensional goals of success; and the authoritative but flexible parenting style of the mother. Clearly Lindsey is paving the way for a social, cultural, and even political conversation long overdue. He is one of the few to have identified the factors pivotal in the lives of many men from female-headed families who have become successful.

After divorcing Michael's father, Michael Lindsey's mother, Charlotte Carter, raised their five sons while employed for nearly a decade as a cafeteria worker—before re-marrying and then going into business as a day-care operator. "Being a single mother, my children never saw me beg. They knew I trusted God for everything, and I let them know that what worked for me could work for them too," Carter says. Her oldest son, Jesse, born when Charlotte was a teenager and raised by her parents, is an oysterman in Virginia. Wesley serves in the army, Ronald is a D.C. corrections officer, David attends Bowie State University on a four-year scholarship, and Gerald died of leukemia in 1989 at the age of twenty-seven. Michael is a social-work professional. Charlotte Carter's sons grew into capable, mature men responsible for themselves and to their community. If she had not been a single mother, her son's achievements might not seem so miraculous.

I was no longer a single mother the day I read a profile of Michael Lindsey and his mother in the *Washington Post,* but I was immediately drawn to the story of both mother and son. The sense of mission and purpose that characterized and joined them resonated in their commentary on their lives. Charlotte Carter and Michael Lindsey symbolized the kind of strength—and the types of men and women who master survival with dignity and grace—that flourishes, but too often goes unhonored, in the black community.

Charlotte Carter's face tells the story of her life. A handsome, sturdy face that is weathered and yet luminous; that bears witness and refuses, out of pride, to reveal everything; her face breaks in the oddest moments into a sly yet strangely innocent smile that seems to surprise her even as she unfurls it. A compact woman, dressed on the day I met her in a colorful pantsuit, she exuded even in repose a penchant and talent for work. Her abundant energy hums quietly like a force field around her.

The living room of her neat three-bedroom bungalow in District Heights, Maryland, is a monument to family and achievement, a space crowded with framed color photos of her sons, posed on graduation days from high school and college, erect in army uniforms, smiling at the camera as they hold her close. Photos line the walls, crowd the mantelpiece, fill the coffee table, flaunting and upholding by their presence what Charlotte Carter believes in most—family and faith and the future, which she nurtures through her love of children. This is the home she lived in and made with her second husband, Perkins Carter, during the four years of their marriage before he died of a brain tumor. A day-care center, a long-cherished dream, is housed in the basement, and Charlotte is a licensed foster mother awaiting approval of her request to formally adopt seven-year-old Jerniece Freeman, whom she took into her home when Jerniece was sixteen months old. A woman possessed of a gift for mothering, Charlotte Carter that day confided in me that she had even thought of opening her home to another foster child.

This comfortable, nearly serene, and satisfying backdrop for her life took years to create, years in which Charlotte Carter walked more than once through interminable darkness. But armed with a steadfast, stubborn will and faith, she always found her way home. Born and raised in the small resort town of Hague, Virginia, to Thomas and Charlotte Smith, Charlotte was one of eleven children. The town was a tourist haven, and her father was a caretaker of the yards and gardens and houses of the wealthy whites who had purchased summer homes there. To provide for his large family, Thomas Smith worked at whatever he could, supplementing his caretaker's salary by digging and shucking oysters to sell. His wife cleaned the houses of the tourist community in the summer.

The Smith family was poor, but the industry of parents and children, the close family ties, the help of good neighbors, and friends all enabled them to get by. Hand-me-down clothes from the white families were accepted with gratitude by Charlotte Smith, even as she lectured her children on the virtues of independence and her belief that hard work could assure the present and build the future. It was a childhood of few frills and no extravagances for the Smith children, but they were cared for and they knew they were loved.

At sixteen, Charlotte became pregnant, and after the

birth of her first son, Jesse, she left Hague and moved to Richmond to work as a live-in domestic worker with a white family, while her parents cared for her son. She moved to Washington, D.C., in 1965, and met and married Clarence Lindsey. Clarence and Charlotte settled on Fort Davis Street in Fairfax Village, a working-class section of Southeast Washington named after the apartment complex that sprawls over much of the area. There they raised their sons, but in 1974, after years of emotional turmoil and economic struggle, they separated. Their last son, David, was conceived during an ill-fated attempt at reconciliation.

Charlotte Carter faced a new world and life with five sons in her care and a minimum-wage job as a cafeteria worker at a neighborhood elementary school. And yet it was during this most difficult time of crisis that she found the twin anchors that would help her through the coming years—religious faith and the institution of the church.

The separation and failed attempt to reconcile took its toll. Traumatized and deeply depressed, Charlotte retreated for emotional support back to her family's home in Hague. When she returned to Washington she checked herself into St. Elizabeth Hospital, the city's public mental health-care facility. But after a night in the facility, Charlotte says, "I got up the next morning and I looked around, and I said no, this ain't the place for me."

In despair one day a few weeks later, Charlotte didn't go to work. She walked to the neighborhood bank, passing Free Gospel Deliverance Temple on the way. "I couldn't drive," she remembers, "so I had to walk everywhere I went. There was a sign in the window of the church that I had seen so many times before, a sign that invited you to come into the church if you were having problems. I had promised myself that one day I would go in. Well, on that day I just felt some power. Some force pulled me into the church. It's like I wasn't even aware of what I was doing. When I came back to myself I was in the front of the church, on my knees praying and crying to the Lord, and I heard this inner voice and I got up and I did what that voice told me to do. I knocked on the door to the pastor's office and I heard a voice from inside say, 'Come in.' I opened the door and I said, 'The Lord told me you can help me.' The pastor, Reverend Ralph E. Green, looked at me and said, 'Sit down, what's your problem?' "

Sitting across from the minister, Charlotte shed tears she didn't know she had left, and told this man who was both pastor and stranger of her fears for herself and her sons, and of her yearning to hold on to the marriage she was losing. The tiny cluttered office became sanctuary and haven. Here she was not judged, only consoled. The shame and confusion, the certainty that she was lost forever, began to dissolve. The sound of her tears, and of her voice revealing all, was a balm. And when Charlotte finished her story and sat trembling, yet sensing a strange calm about to unfold inside her—the pastor asked that they pray together for her to be strengthened, and for her to know what to do and where to go in her search for peace of mind.

Reverend Green asked her to return for the Tuesday night service. Charlotte remembers, "I was there just like he asked me to be, and he prayed for me. After he prayed for me, he put his hands on my shoulders and gave me a push and said, 'Go, now run for your life.' And that's when I really started seeking the Lord. After he prayed for me I felt like it gave me a new life, a new hope, a new everything." In the months and years that followed, healing began. Charlotte realized that reconciliation with Clarence Lindsey was neither possible nor in the best interests of herself and her sons. Her faith had endowed her with the vision with which to assess herself, her husband, and their union. What she had once seen as the end of her life, she now knew was the beginning.

Religious faith became the guiding principle that shaped Charlotte's parenting ethic, and gave her strength. The church became an all-encompassing part of her life and the lives of her sons. Church attendance was mandatory—every Sunday, and three days a week during revivals.

After her separation and divorce, Charlotte received a modest amount of child support, but even combined with her salary, there never seemed to be enough money to care for her family. "Sometimes things were tough," she says. "I've had my water cut off because I wasn't at home at the right time to pay it. I didn't have the money to pay it but would work something out so I could pay the bill over time. There were times when I took one pound of bacon and fed the kids one week off of it. But we had food. The food that

I cooked. Never expensive food. We never went out to dinner. One year, I'll never forget, I didn't have money to buy
a Christmas tree, and the kids were so sad and so pitiful, so
I went to the store and it just so happened that I found a
little silver tree, about four feet tall, on sale, and I bought
that. And I brought it home and sat it on the table. I told
them that was all the Christmas tree I could afford that
year.

"There have been so many times when forces were clos-
ing in on me as a single parent, telling me, 'You're going to
be nothing.' And I had to fight over that force and get to
God, to the one who I knew would take me over. I have
been in tight situations. I went on welfare one time; that
was when I was pregnant with David and I wasn't working,
and I couldn't get support for him from his father like I
wanted to, and I couldn't work. So for five months I went
on public assistance. But as soon as I was able to get off, I
did, and started taking care of myself." Periodically, Charlotte supplemented her salary from the elementary school
with domestic work.

"I've been in the church for nineteen years and I never
asked the church for no help of no kind, to pay my rent,
buy food, nothing. I sought God for everything. And I'm
not patting myself on the back but it all goes to God,
raising up my children by myself with no husband, and I
did better than some families with a man in the house. And
I sit sometimes and I just praise God because I know that it
was Him that did it."

Charlotte's faith also buttressed her determination to save her sons from the snare of negative elements in their neighborhood. She broke up fights between her sons and other boys, marched down to the neighborhood recreation center if the boys stayed out past curfew and dragged them home. Charlotte was feared and respected on Fort Davis Street, acting as mother and father with the help of God. And her strong sense of independence meant that she rarely asked her family back in Hague for help.

When I asked Charlotte how her sons became men, she told me without hesitation. "By seeing me strong. They looked at the inner strength within me.

"I've always been strong on discipline. But there is a difference between being with somebody and being with nobody. When I was with nobody I felt like I had to stand even stronger, because I had to do everything then. I'm the mother, I'm the father. I'm the provider, I'm the disciplinarian. I'm everything. I had to do everything and it just made me stronger."

At Free Gospel Deliverance Temple the congregation worshiped God with a mighty roar and a bursting heart, with tambourines, shouts of ecstasy, tears, and a collective, thunderous voice of praise. This was no-holds-barred worship; nothing held back love of God the Father as patriarch and creator. Free Gospel Deliverance Temple became a spiritual citadel of strength and hope for Charlotte and her sons. Waking each morning to another day as primary emotional and material support for her children, Charlotte could call on the confidence that was buttressed and nourished by her religious conviction. In Charlotte's world—as she hurried to dress for work, gave her sons their tasks for that morning, and left the house—she knew that, no matter what, she was not alone. The God she believed in was present in all the houses on Fort Davis Street, and especially in the home she made with her sons. Although the struggle to hold on to the house, and to give the boys everything they needed, was often overwhelming, every time she "got over" another hurdle, improvised a bridge to cross a new dilemma stretched before her, made do and made a way, Charlotte felt stronger. Everyone was suffering in that house, the boys unsure of their father's love, Charlotte eternally worried that she could not adequately provide for them, vowing every day not to lose the boys to the streets, never able to be weak for one minute. But all this kept providing her with ways to grow strong—and each time she felt strong, she felt God. Because there were so many demands and she had to have so much faith, Charlotte felt strong more often than anyone would ever believe.

In the church, Charlotte and her sons had a family. Active in several clubs, and the initiator of numerous projects at Free Gospel Deliverance Temple, Charlotte gradually acquired a reputation among the young people of the church as a trusted, compassionate counselor and advisor—someone they could talk to who would listen, and whose words could make a difference. Young people came to Charlotte with their problems. She listened to them and she prayed with and for them. Even as she prayed for others, she included prayers to realize her own dreams. She didn't want to be a cafeteria worker all her life. Sometimes, on her way to work or whenever her mind was free of worries, she fantasized about having her own nursery school or day-care center. She was so good with children, and working with them tapped into and brought out talents and satisfactions that few other endeavors inspired. Everyone said she had a gift. But where would the money come from? Charlotte didn't know. But God surely hadn't given her a gift that would go unused.

Of her sons, only Michael really loved the church like she did, felt the faith deep inside. But the other boys were being saved even when they complained of having to dress up (in the suits and ties and white shirts she got on sale at Morton's) and parade past their friends to the bus stop on Sunday morning. It didn't matter if they failed to understand this. For in the church on Sunday they saw faith-filled men and women. And Charlotte was especially grateful that inside the walls of her church her boys saw men, men who were there as surrogate fathers for Wesley, Gerald, David, Ronald, and Michael, anytime she called. They'd thank her one day, she knew her sons would. And they would thank God, too.

Her faith wasn't a one-day-a-week performance. She was

up against the nitty-gritty of life seven days a week, and her faith was both all and everything she had. Monday morning was as sacred as Sunday morning. For each day had been created by God, and each day was another chance to serve her God by loving her sons and herself.

∽

THE DAY MICHAEL LINDSEY entered my house, I knew that I was in the presence of a deeply spiritual and gifted young person. At twenty-four he had shaved his head, which accentuated his large, calm but inquisitive eyes. I could feel and sense the nearly combustible energy beneath the surface. He was mannerly and soft-spoken, but his words were chosen for accuracy and he seemed to have thought out every response. He was, in the words of black folklore, an old spirit.

Michael was working then as a psychotherapist with a mental health center, and with another therapist running a support group for single mothers who were residents of a D.C. housing project. Over herbal tea and zucchini bread our conversation that day ranged over a host of topics, from his education to his family and his father. He gave me a copy of his master's thesis, and I read in the early pages the following: "If one out of every twenty-two African American males will be killed by violent crime, what about the other twenty-one? If one out of every six African American males will be arrested by the time they reach the age of nineteen, what about the other five? And finally, if one out of every four African American males are presently incarcerated, what about the other three? This study comes from a strength perspective, one that emphasizes the positive qualities and attributes of the human experience."

But during our initial conversation I had sensed the wellspring of pain that existed beside the resilience that activated much of Michael's quest for truth and identity. He had sought out the men in his study because he was clearly seeking to know himself as well. He worked in the healing art of mental health because in his own way he was seeking to heal the wounds inflicted by his absent father. I had heard and seen and sensed optimism motivated by a deep sense of tragedy, strength, and vulnerability.

Fort Davis Street is lined with neat row houses ending in a cul-de-sac. The Fort Davis Recreation Center sits on the edge of the cul-de-sac and during the 1980s was a centerpiece of Mayor Marion Barry's outreach efforts to the city's youth. With a variety of educational and mentoring programs, including guaranteed summer jobs for youth, the mayor had made the city's young a top priority. Michael remembers that it wasn't uncommon to see the mayor, accompanied by aides, show up at the rec center to toss a ball with the young boys, or shoot hoops in the time-honored tradition of the savvy politician. Southeast Washington, with its disproportionately high rates of social ills, crime, and poverty, had long been a bastion of support for the mayor—who had early in his career cast himself as both a rebel against the establishment and a "down brother" most at home with the people on the streets of Southeast, whom he would never forget.

The years of Michael's childhood also witnessed the beginning of the infiltration of drugs into black communities. A family on Fort Davis Street headed a drug ring. The street, like many that were home to black families, suffered its share of casualties of the drug wars. At the rec center, while teens shot hoops, groups of older men shot craps and smoked marijuana. The rec center was the nerve center for the neighborhood youth, but Charlotte, fearing the possible dangers of temptation, allowed her sons to go to there only in the daytime. The streetlights flickering on was the sign that the Lindsey boys' curfew was in effect.

"She was firm about not losing us to the streets," Michael says. "That was her goal. Over and over she told us, 'I will not lose you to the streets.' " Even as Charlotte worked to ensure her sons' safety, she could not shield them from the often lethal conflicts that ensnared their friends. "I'd be talking to guys one day, and then the next day or even that evening hear that they'd been shot or gotten killed," Michael remembers. "It was really frightening as a young person knowing that people had been shot on my street or near my house."

As a result, Michael grew cautious, conservative. Unlike the other teens who frequented parties and outdoor Go-Go concerts (a brand of music honed on the streets of Southeast, heavy on a pulsing drumbeat), Michael stayed home on the weekends studying—mostly, he says, because "I wanted to live."

Michael was chided by his brothers as being Charlotte's favorite, and it is clear that there is a powerful symbiosis, an awesome bond between mother and son. Michael shares his mother's deep-rooted religious faith and conviction, her compassion for others, and sense of duty to community. In school Michael was studious, serious, and sought to shine. In elementary school he was on the student council; in junior high school he served as student council president, captain of the basketball team, and was considered an exceptional student. When challenged to fight by fellow students, Michael says, he chose to respond nonviolently, fearing his mother's wrath more than any punishment a bully could impose.

But Michael's ability to cope with the challenges and the traumas of Fort Davis Street did not blind him to other realities. "In junior high, around the time I was thirteen, that was when I first began to recognize that we lacked certain material things," he says. "I saw the other kids with nice clothes, name-brand jeans and sneakers. We didn't have as much. I convinced myself that I'd be able to get those things in the future. I thought if I stayed out of trouble and did well academically, everything that I wanted would be mine at a later date." Michael is a young man who, at a very young age, tapped into the spiritual resources of an inner life that would serve and save him.

Remembering his childhood church attendance, Michael says, "Mom didn't have a car in those days, so we walked to church, and as we passed by the kids outside playing on Sunday morning, seeing us dressed in suits and ties, we'd get teased." *Here come the Lindsey boys* was the refrain that trailed Charlotte and her sons as they marched to Free Gospel Deliverance Temple.

Yet, while some kids teased them, Michael remembers some of the older boys in the neighborhood—and even the drug dealers—admonishing their tormentors, "Them boys going to be something because their mother always got them going to church." In the embrace of Free Gospel Deliverance Temple, Michael found a congregation that supported a variety of programs for youth. The church owned property in rural Virginia, and the young boys of the congregation were often taken there for weekend retreats where older male members held workshops and group discussions about peer pressure, the responsibilities of adulthood, and holding on to Christian values.

Michael grew to love the church deeply and was molded by it in ways more pronounced than his brothers were. "As a Pentecostal church, the service is charismatic, expressive," he explains. "All this was at odds with the traditional definitions of masculinity and manhood, and gave me a rich opportunity to express emotions about my love of and dedication to God, and to legitimize emotional expression in other areas of my life.

"My mother was a solid force in our lives, exemplifying a

work ethic, a strong belief in faith and God, and also love, nurturing, and the support a parent should give to a child. I didn't see having been raised in a single-parent home as an obstacle to anything I wanted to be."

But Michael was not always so sure. He shared with me his struggle to overcome the hidden yet deep-seated anger he often felt. "I was angry because of the situation I grew up in. I've always wanted to have a father around but didn't. I was angry about our economic situation, I was angry because the guys I knew at fifteen and sixteen were riding around in Mercedes Benzes, BMWs, and I didn't, and I was always trying to do the right thing and wondered why it was like that. I was angry because guys got killed, my friends got killed, just angry. And often when I was younger I was ready to take my anger out on people at any time."

At one point in high school Michael carried a gun for protection; and while an undergraduate at Morehouse, after one of his classmates was robbed and beaten the first day of school, Michael thought again of carrying a gun but realized he could not, because "I had no intention of really using it," and his brother Ronald had warned him not to carry a gun unless he could pull the trigger.

Still, in every assessment of who he has become and who he may one day be, Michael always returns to the legacy of his mother. "I have seen from my mother that a woman is capable of holding her own," he concludes. "My mother expanded my definition of what a woman is capable of doing, and I am willing to give leeway to whatever my wife wants to do and not feel inferior as a man.

"The way I grew up has in a sense become a crusade, it's given me a lot of impetus to be a success. I feel like I have a calling. The research and the writing I'm doing is my way of making sense of all this."

"You learn how much you have been loved through loving a child. So many times with Azulai, I've had flashbacks to those women who raised me, to how they loved me and how that affected the way I love her; and none of them had husbands and none of them suffered from it."

CLAUDIA BOOKER WAS raised in a house of women, a home that was matriarchal and that celebrated and exemplified the strengths of women as mothers and creators of their own destiny. The independence, resilience, and fortitude Claudia saw in the lives of her female kin made a way for the former judge and one-time member of the staff of President Jimmy Carter to imagine and then to know that she could choose and create her fate no matter what. Claudia, in making the choice to become a single mother through adoption, was a forerunner, an explorer—as in many of her life choices. An effervescent, charismatic woman, Claudia is as much warrior as mother. The grand gesture, the total commitment, and the passionately held belief have been the hallmarks of her life, personally and professionally. Hold nothing back. *Ask everything, because that's what I will give* could well be her creed. Possessed of a huge hunger for life, knowledge, and love, Claudia's journey from the house of women on Cleveland's Superior Avenue, where black female strength protected and shaped her, to her own art-filled condominium in Washington, D.C., where she parents her daughter, Azulai, and herself, has been a journey defined by plumbing of the depths and discarding fear and doubt. She has been lost but more often found, and, when wrong, braver than she may have had a right to be. Her conversations can zoom from a wickedly derisive yet informed and astute analysis of the Byzantine world of local politics, to a discourse on Yoruba religion, to the stories behind each of the striking paintings that fill her home, evidence of her passion for art.

The Superior Avenue neighborhood, which Claudia remembers as "blue collar/no collar," was largely working class. "In kindergarten it was mostly Jewish, and by the time I was in first grade it was all black." The house on that street—which became home for Claudia and her mother in the aftermath of her parents' separation—was inhabited by several generations of amazing women. There was "Muddy Dear," Claudia's widowed great grandmother; her daughter "Mama Teenie," divorced and, in the euphemism of the era, a "practical nurse" who cared for the children of wealthy white clients in their homes; "Aunt Rickey," Mama Teenie's sister, also divorced, and employed by the Veterans

Administration; and Claudia's mother's sister, "Aunt Dee Dee," unmarried and an employee of the telephone company. All the women pooled their resources and were collectively paying for the house on Superior Avenue.

This was the house that Claudia's mother sent her to from Washington, D.C., while she finalized her separation from Claudia's father, a medical student at Howard University. "A year later," Claudia remembers, "Mother came and joined the crew." It was a house of strong-willed, opinionated women about whom Claudia says, "None of them had husbands and none of them suffered from it.

"It was absolutely electric, growing up in that house. Things were always just one step from vibrant. At the breakfast table there'd be major discussion over what goes on the cereal first, sugar or milk, and each woman had a different philosophy of life and concept of how I should be raised." But despite the divergence in parenting styles, Claudia says her five mothers all taught her how to be independent. "Things were so complete in that house, there was just no space for men to occupy. These women didn't feel men as absent or their lives as less valuable because there weren't men around. Aunt Dee Dee had a boyfriend, and there were men friends and family members that came through. I saw my father in the summers and I was very close to my grandfather, but I never felt like my aunts and grandmothers needed them to be real, to be complete. And all of the women finger-popped, partied, loved life, and valued their connections with other women."

Mama Teenie would bring home bounties of treasure from the houses she worked in. "When Mama Teenie came home with her shopping bag, we knew she'd be bringing something good, and exciting—fresh asparagus (we always ate it from the can) fresh mushrooms—and she'd exclaim about her employers, 'No child needs forty pairs of socks!' and hand me a pair. There were always nearly new clothes for me that the white families got tired of wearing. I always felt like Mama Teenie was just redistributing the wealth." But more important, Claudia knew that in the homes of her wealthy clients Mama Teenie was often forced to swallow her pride when treated with disrespect, yet "she taught me to be proud, and that you don't always have to declare war on everybody to make your point."

In an effort to bring a sense of dignity to a job too often deemed merely menial, and also to forge bonds of sisterhood, Mama Teenie and a dozen other women who did domestic work formed a social club. Once a month a different woman would host the group, inviting the club into her home for games of bid whist or bridge, and luncheons that featured elegant canapés and hors d'oeuvres, sumptuous éntrées, and tables laden with the kind of fine china, flatware, and linen (often handed down by employers) that the women cleaned and polished in their employers' homes. At these monthly gatherings the women danced with each other to Sam Cooke, Sarah Vaughan, Jackie Wilson, Nat King Cole, and the Platters, cut their employers down to size in evaluations of character as accurate as any Rorschach test, kicked off their shoes as they sipped sherry or downed a shot of scotch, bathed each other in melodious, raucous laughter reserved for such occasions, shared secrets, and sought advice. Claudia remembers that, although she was consigned to the kitchen to help clean and serve because the living room on those nights was off limits to children, "Even then it seemed to me that in those moments for those women their universe was complete." Sneaking a glance into the living room whenever she could, eagerly listening for the ribald joke, the squeal of laughter, or more important, the hushed silence that signaled something she really *had* to hear, Claudia says, "I learned that women could be whole, that their lives could be intrinsically full, just by being women, just as they were."

The lessons Claudia learned in that house were persistent and embedded in everything the women did. And one of the things those women did, with skill and diligence and creativity, was work. "The women in my family didn't sit around and wait for things to come to them. They didn't wait for anybody. They went out and got what they wanted. They always worked, were always busy, but never complained about being tired or defeated."

These women taught Claudia crucial lessons. From Muddy Dear, her great-grandmother, Claudia learned the meaning of absolute, unconditional love. "Muddy Dear was consistent in her love and in her punishment. There were simply rules of society and rules of the family that I had to obey, and if I didn't there were consequences to pay and the consequences were swift. And yet after I got a beating, which I inevitably deserved, and knew I would get, Muddy Dear hugged me, ordered me to dry my tears, clean myself up, and go make a butter and sugar sandwich. She taught me that in life there were rewards and punishments, and that after you were punished for infractions you just went on with your life."

Aunt Rickey was the family curmudgeon, hard to please, quick to criticize, a taskmaster, but Claudia remembers that it was she who often gave her a bath—gently rubbing her back, washing her until she was clean after she'd come in the house dirty from a day of summer play—revealing in those moments a tender, loving side. It was Aunt Rickey who bought Claudia a United States Savings Bond on the day she was born, and who bought her at least one every year after that, hoping to ensure her niece's future financial security.

Aunt Dee Dee was the one Claudia could always talk to when no one else understood, the one who took her to the playground and who enjoyed pushing her on the swing, watching her slide down the sliding board, talking to her niece as though Claudia was an adult, not a child. It was Aunt Dee Dee who knew her deepest secrets, and her fears.

Claudia's mother, Shirley, dropped out of Howard University in her sophomore year to help support her husband, Clifford Booker, whom she had met when she was fifteen and married at nineteen. While Clifford studied at Howard and worked three jobs of his own, Shirley worked at the then War Department, now Defense Department, as a secretary to support the family. But by the time Clifford entered medical school, the marriage had dissolved.

Returning to Cleveland, Shirley enrolled at Western Reserve University (now Case Western Reserve), where she pursued and ultimately earned a degree in musicology and education, which led to a thirty-year career teaching in Cleveland's public schools. To support herself and Claudia, and to help with the communal expenses of the female extended family, Shirley, while in college, waited tables at exclusive country clubs outside Cleveland. She even sold a famous hair-care product of the fifties for men, going from beauty shop to barber shop in the city's black community to sell Nu Nile hair pomade. When there still wasn't enough money, she went to Atlantic City and worked as a bartender during the summer; and she sang in clubs. From her mother Claudia learned the value of hard work, that it was rewarded, and that it generated pride and independence.

She learned also to appreciate beauty and culture. Shirley played the piano for relaxation, often singing the wry, witty songs of Bobby Short and Mabel Mercer. She wrote her own songs and collected antiques. The year Claudia was ten, Shirley saved for a year to buy tickets to take Claudia to see a Metropolitan Opera performance in Cleveland of *La Bohème,* a tradition that Claudia continued with Azulai. "I had gone kicking and screaming, fighting all the way to see the opera that day," Claudia remembers. "I wanted to go to the movies instead but my mother dragged me into the concert hall, and when the lights went up and the first note filled the air I was speechless."

The women of the house on Superior Avenue brought an artistry, intelligence, and spirit to their lives that indelibly shaped the little girl growing up in their midst. Because they clearly felt that a woman's place was wherever she wanted to be, Claudia grew into a woman for whom exemplary professional achievement was expected and attained. Since the women modeled a collective, almost communal style of parenting, Claudia was raised with a healthy sense of single parenting as a possibility. In the days of Claudia's childhood, the term "single parent" had not been coined. This was simply the way many women lived.

Claudia went on to do herself and the women on Superior Avenue proud. A product of the late sixties' influences, from Black Pride and Black Power to feminism, Claudia grew into a New World Woman. Affirmative Action, the Sexual Revolution, the Pill, the emergence of African nations from colonialism, were among the forces that shaped Claudia as a student at the University of Hartford in Connecticut, where she received her B.A. Now the walls were tumbling down, were being blown up by black and white and colored people who were dreamers of a new great society. Claudia, armed with the confidence that had been her inheritance, strode through every door she encountered and sat down at the table as though women who looked like her had always been there.

After college she spent a year working with emotionally challenged ninth graders in science. She picked up a master's degree in Urban Education, also from the University of Hartford, and got her law degree from Northeastern University in Boston; then, on her way to Kano, a city in northern Nigeria to teach law under the auspices of a United Nations program, she stopped off in Washington, D.C. Claudia wanted, she says, "to make a difference and to be around black people." Impressed with the city's large black population and the opportunities it offered, she decided not to go to Nigeria but to stay in D.C. There followed positions with the United States Commission on Civil Rights, the District of Columbia Bar Association, the Carter White House, and the Federal Railroad Administration at the Department of Transportation, where she supervised the design and construction of Amtrak stations along the Northeast corridor. Claudia's work was important, and as a strong, outspoken, well-educated, high-salaried, professional black woman cutting a swath through the halls of both local and federal bureaucracies, she found ample opportunities to make a difference.

In her career, the work she enjoyed most was that which pushed her to the limit, provided pressure, required that she think on her feet, use her instincts. During her two years in the Carter White House doing advance work, Claudia arranged the president's tour of Three Mile Island after the nuclear meltdown had occurred, planned his trip to Mt. Saint Helens in Washington when the volcano had exploded, and traveled as part of the team accompanying Carter at the SALT talks to stop nuclear proliferation.

It seemed that she had it all. But something was still missing. When I asked Claudia to tell me why she decided to adopt, she answered by telling me about a brief two-year marriage inspired by her desire to "get married to have children." Motherhood was always part of the plan. At one point she had considered becoming a doctor, like her father, but after enrolling in a premed program, Claudia dropped out because she felt there was no way that the rigors of the profession would allow her to be a doctor, a wife, and a mother. Although Claudia had been raised quite successfully by her mother, she easily admits now, blessed with twenty-twenty hindsight, that she chose her husband "because I thought he'd be a great dad, someone who'd be a good father." The incompatibilities, however, were major and stark and bloomed for Claudia to see in the first hours of the honeymoon. Counseling only revealed why the marriage couldn't work. They parted as friends.

The seeds of this desire to find a perfect father for the child she was determined to have were planted in the conflicted, often unfulfilling relationship with her father, a man who married eight times and whom Claudia describes as a "tempestuous womanizer" who couldn't handle emotional intimacy. But Clifford Booker was also her father, the man she loved, and forgave over and over, whose legacy she struggled with and who inspired the greatest gift she would ultimately give to her adopted daughter, Azulai. More than Claudia wanted a life partner, she wanted a man who would be to *her* child the father Clifford Booker never was to her.

"I was thirty-five when I adopted Azulai, and I was at a point in my life where I had done it all. I was a lawyer, and as a single woman I lived a very self-absorbed life. I'd take a week off from my job and fly to the Bahamas or Paradise Island. I was partying a lot, dating lots of guys, I knew and had dated loads of NBA basketball players, had two closets full of clothes. I'd been to Brazil, to Carnaval; you name it, I had done it. But even as I was doing all that I wanted something deeper, and motherhood is as deep as it gets. I had realized that my career as a lawyer really wasn't going to fulfill me in the ways I had thought it would. Being professionally successful didn't give me as much as I had expected. I often say that Azulai saved my life because when I adopted her there was no way that the excesses of my former lifestyle could exist. That lifestyle ended and another door opened.

"I didn't think my parents could handle me going out and getting pregnant by some 'Disco Dan' just passing through my life, and that meant a lot to me and that's why I chose to adopt. There is of course the ego gratification involved in being able to look at a child and see your genes and your imprint and say, 'I did that.' But that wasn't so important to me. I wanted to be some little girl's mother. I wanted a tiny baby. I wanted to be involved in a child's life right from the beginning.

"There were some weird things in the adoption process. When I contacted the public agencies here in D.C., I found that as a single parent I could get a 'special needs' child or a child with a sibling, but my chances of getting a healthy, so-called 'perfect' child were small because they were given to two-parent families. That made no sense to me. Why give a single parent with one income all the children with the greatest material and emotional needs? So then I found a private agency that specialized in African American children. When they asked me what personality traits I wanted the child to have, I said my only two requirements were that the child be quick-minded and fearless. I come from a fast-talking, witty, funny, loquacious family, and you've got to be able to hold your own with them, that was my only concern. Other than that, I didn't care what she looked like and all the rest. Azulai tested very high on the tests given to gauge the baby's response to stimuli when they are born, so she was clearly sharp.

"When you adopt a child you have to write an essay about why you're doing this, why you want a child, what a child will give you. You really have to think about it and justify your desire to be a parent. It's actually a healthy process, I think. In my essay I wrote that I wanted a daughter because I had a lot of love and energy I wanted to give to someone else. I had been a Big Sister and had seen how loving someone unconditionally could change a child's life. I wanted to do that on a consistent basis. Also I believe that children keep you young, and I was ready for a new challenge.

"The agency in Dallas, Texas, called me on a Tuesday night to tell me that the adoption had been finalized and they wanted me to come to get Azulai on Saturday. I didn't even have a Pamper in the house, but friends from my job gave me everything I needed. A crib, clothes, a car seat, everything. I'll never forget the scene at the airport. I hadn't expected it to happen like this, but I walked off the plane and within a few moments I was met by a lady from the adoption agency who asked me if I was Claudia Booker. When I said that I was, she just put Azulai in my arms and just like that I was a mother. The foster mother and her children were there, they were crying, the lady from the adoption agency was in tears, and so was I. I signed the papers and caught the next plane back to Washington."

Claudia named her daughter Canida, her great-grandparents' last name; Azulai, a Cape Verdean name; Mandela, after the South African freedom fighters Winnie and Nelson; Booker; and, as part of her transition to motherhood, she took three months off from her job as a lawyer with the Department of Transportation.

"My father was a pediatrician, so he was a lot of help, and he put me in touch with a network of older 'wise women' who had raised their kids and their kids' kids and knew everything about child rearing, and they helped me get through all the stages. When I took the time off, it was just me and Azulai for the first two weeks, then my grandmother came for a month. It's been a tradition that, since Azulai was young, I get a month vacation that she spends with my family in Cleveland. And my girlfriends who also had kids have helped me out so much, especially in learning which battles with Azulai to fight and which ones to let go of.

"I wasn't prepared for how consuming the job of motherhood is. My first Christmas after adopting Azulai, my mom asked me what I wanted for Christmas. I told her I wanted to be able to sleep until one o'clock in the afternoon. And that's what my mom gave me, she took care of Azulai so I got to sleep late for a couple of days. Yet I didn't begrudge Azulai the lack of sleep. Being somebody's mother means giving what you don't know you have, giving from a place you didn't know was there. Being somebody's mother is serious business. You have to carefully consider it. We spend more time choosing a car than choosing a mate or even thinking about parenthood. Being a parent causes you to assess yourself in ways that are often not comfortable, but you have to do it anyway. And you have to put yourself last for many years. There's no such thing as 'I have a right to a life too.'

"Sometimes Azulai will say to me, when I'm telling her that she has to advocate and fight for herself and her rights, 'But you're so strong.' I tell her that I didn't start out that way, that my mother and relatives taught me to be strong.

She's seen me over and over again handle situations force-fully on her behalf, and I'm trying to teach her what I was taught. I tell her that you have to be persistent and strong. I want her to see this as a strategy for life, not just a reaction. One summer the school bus was later and later every morning for a week, coming to pick her up for summer school, and every time I spoke with the person who scheduled the bus about it, nothing happened; so one day I walked Azulai out to the bus stop and got on the bus and told the bus driver politely but forcefully, energetically but without using bad language, that I was tired of the bus being late, and that I was going downtown that day to complain to the superintendent. That afternoon I did just that. I wasn't able to see the superintendent but I made my point, and the point I wanted to make for Azulai, which was to stand up for herself and get what she deserves."

Claudia's decision to become a mother, a *single mother,* through adoption is the kind of choice that speaks volumes about the changing, expanding lives of contemporary women. Women have informally adopted, taken children in need into their homes, and acted as substitute mothers for countless generations. So the altruistic, maternal impulse that motivated Claudia to adopt Azulai is ancient and represents the timeless desire to love and be loved, to protect and nurture. Single women like Claudia are making a statement about the totality of their lives when they adopt. These women are throwing off the centuries-old belief that a woman's life can begin, her deepest desires be made manifest, her need to be a mother can be fulfilled only after she has become a man's wife. For Claudia and the thousands of single women who adopt each year, the presence of a man as husband and father is no longer a prerequisite for motherhood and family. As much as these women, like Andrea, simply "get tired of waiting" for a life partner, they are—even more important—eager to take their lives into their own hands. Often these are women who have careers as opposed to jobs, and who have made a practice of shattering conventional wisdom. Single-parent motherhood then becomes not an exceptional choice but a decision consistent with, and that grows out of, all the other most important decisions they have made.

The adoptive single mother is scrutinized, tested, and assessed in ways that women who conceive a child are not. In many cases the adoptive mother knows that one day her child will seek out her biological mother; in Claudia's case she feels it is necessary for her to facilitate Azulai's process of coming to terms with that part of her past. This is single motherhood that is complicated but no less fulfilling than the experience of birth mothers. It is motherhood that still allows Claudia Booker to conclude, "Being a mother causes you to recall how you were loved by your family. You learn how much you have been loved through loving a child. So many times with Azulai I've had flashbacks to those women who raised me, to how they loved me and how that affected the way I love her."

"See me? I am a fragmented woman, as are all the mothers I know. Indistinctly lovely, frightening, disoriented, and sometimes dangerous up close."

WHEN I MET Janet Maloney Franze, she was giving painful, unexpected, yet quite wonderful birth to herself. In the midst of a separation from her husband that would transform her from affluent suburban soccer mom to divorced single mother/graduate student/writer/teacher/feminist, she was a woman who cherished every moment of motherhood and was learning how to mother herself, and to give voice to instincts that the love of her children had taught her finally to trust.

Motherhood. Therapy. Divorce. These became the passages to a woman self hidden behind the mask of baby girl/good girl/*A* student/dutiful wife/supermom. As a graduate student in a nonfiction writing workshop I was teaching at

Virginia Commonwealth University, Janet was the only member of the class who wanted to write about motherhood, about outlining papers in feminist literary theory in her head while combing her daughter's hair. In a class of poets and novelists and memoirists and wordsmiths practiced in the art of shredding the soul to feed the imagination, Janet was more than a little afraid. She had dissected the intent, the themes in the lives of fictional women rendered unforgettable by Jane Austen, George Sand, and Virginia Woolf. There was always the protective seal of the jargon of literary criticism, the intellectual distance required by the need for objectivity and the requisite footnotes used to validate every assertion. But Janet had signed up for my class, although she didn't know it at first, because she was ready to write about someone real, someone flesh and blood. She wanted to write about herself.

Everything was falling apart and being remade. A thirteen-year marriage, in which she had been corporate wife but never herself, was deconstructing like some once-cherished natural law proven by progress to be entirely unsupportable. Each week in the class she wrote more, dug deeper, and I could almost see the flakes of skin she shed. Of course the paper in its first incarnation was academic—that was her most familiar, sanctioned voice—an examination of the role and symbolism of motherhood in the fiction of several women writers.

Janet would soon be a divorced, single mother. Her children, Nathan and Jenna, were angry, confused, didn't understand what was happening. She had been back in school a year, a decision that, like the choice to have her children, saved her life. The rigors of the academy, the new friends, the rediscovery of the intellectual life buoyed her, and confirmed the voice at the center of the domestic life that she had tried to hold on to but that had slipped away. In her first efforts in my class, she wrote about other women writers, anybody but herself. But the essay found its way, as it had to, into the region of her untold story, scratching and kicking and screaming inside her for its own messy but necessary life. Nathan's and Jenna's and her own fears and excitement, the rush and the madness and the beauty of motherhood, kept drowning out the proper Victorian lady writers, most of whom had never been mothers anyway. In the end Janet fomented a coup, overthrew the stories that had already been told, and wrote her own instead:

I loved that first pregnancy. Never had I felt more real, more there. Twitches metamorphosed into discernible body parts under my hands, my heart burned, my stomach heaved. The more bizarre it became, the more melded I felt. I had a purpose. I had status. Once, miserable and uncomfortable and huge, I said "screw it" and parked in the handicapped space nearest the drugstore. One glance at me heading toward him and the cop tore up the ticket he'd been writing. Pregnancy was power. If I write what I know, I write motherhood. If I read what I know, I read motherhood. If I walk, talk and eat what I know, I walk with a child on my hip. I talk in a high, engage-the-baby voice, and I eat gone-cold food while I pour cups of apple juice. In short, sudden moments of suspended animation—between the second I notice all is calm and the next second when all isn't—I wonder what happened to what I used to know. I wonder if it matters. If it ever mattered.

The story begins in Canton, Ohio—small town, middle America, industrial, home of the Football Hall of Fame. In Janet's own words, "A white-bread town, a white-bread life, a white-bread girl." White-bread, functional, middle of the road, normal, and in the back of her mind Janet always feared "unremarkable." She was the baby of a family of five children raised in a warm, traditional Irish Catholic family. Mom stayed home. Dad ran his own business, a general rental store, that rented everything from party supplies to lawn mowers. "I was the peacemaker, the mediator, the good girl," she remembers with a grimace that seems to indict that role. Years of therapy have uncovered the need, expressed in finely tuned ambassadorial skills, to keep peace at any cost, because if something happened that she couldn't predict or control, then everyone might find out what she thought was true, that she wasn't really smart, she wasn't really nice. She was always harder on herself than anyone else could be. As the youngest of five children, Janet watched her siblings take risks, and she vowed never to repeat their mistakes, never to draw attention to herself. What she feared most was recognition, for it might reveal that she wasn't worthy, didn't deserve all the attention.

But even as a child Janet had wanted to write, had hoarded her passion for language like a delicious secret whose whims she would gladly obey. But for years she was afraid to discover that she couldn't write well, so she didn't. The power of words, the awesome responsibility they imposed, the doors they opened, all that was more than she could bear. On the rare occasions that she did write, often she couldn't handle what words set in motion. For Mother's Day it was she who her brothers and sisters forced to compose poems and songs celebrating their mother. When Mom broke down in tears of gratitude and happiness, the emotion pushed Janet back into her shell. In school her essays and poems mostly brought ringing praise from the nuns. Janet refused to believe their praise was genuine, but the rare criticism she could handle, for that sounded more right. More true.

Good grades came easy, but she didn't really believe she was as smart as she clearly was. She graduated cum laude from Ohio University and was married a year later, to Harry, who had attended the same high school, had known her older brother, was a friend of mutual friends. The transitions were safe, secure—college, then marriage. There had never been a space or place of her own. There had never been the need for such a thing. Janet lived at home, went to college, then made her own home with a husband. This was right, this was natural, this was the way it was supposed to be.

Harry, whom she married nine months after they met at

a party, struck Janet as a rebel. He rode a motorcycle and nurtured his wild side, even while working in his family's business, a shop that made parts for manufacturing machines. Janet loved his intensity. "I knew the minute I saw Harry when he walked into the party, disheveled, in his work clothes, a little dirty but not really caring, that I'd marry him. He told his friends I swept him off his feet." Harry was eager to leave the family business and go out on his own. Janet didn't have a job. In love, the world seemed to be theirs to design, so they planned to move to California. They got married because there was no way her parents would have accepted them living together.

But before they could leave for California, Harry was hired by General Electric and they moved to Cleveland. Looking back, Janet concludes, "I met a guy just like my dad and got married." Harry's impressive administrative and business skills were recognized and nurtured at GE, and Harry became one of the youngest plant managers in the company's history. But the fast track took its toll in long hours. Harry often worked from 6 A.M. to 7 P.M. while Janet worked first at Stouffer's and then Nestle's in public relations. The closeness and intimacy, the shared life Janet thought marriage guaranteed, didn't materialize.

Early on, Janet and Harry had decided to wait five years before having children, and although when the five years were up, and Janet felt the marriage was dead, she still wanted to become a mother. "I didn't think having children would save the marriage but I knew it would save me," she says. Nathan was her firstborn. "Something happened when Nathan was born. I nursed him a long time, until he was two. I loved the connectedness that I felt with him. Nursing him that long was what I needed, it was what he needed. I mothered from my gut. I had always been good at instinctual things, and I had always felt somehow that I would be a really good mother. When my kids were born, after a while I began to feel like I could follow my instincts, follow an instinctive spiritual path in my whole life. And I felt like the only time in my marriage that Harry was un-equivocally proud of me was when I gave birth to my son. In so many other areas of the marriage I always felt that Harry was in charge, I could be overruled on the slightest thing; but motherhood was my domain, he couldn't really take over there."

A year after Nathan was born, Harry was hired for an even higher-level manufacturing job with AMF in Rich-mond, Virginia. While Harry looked for a house, Janet and Nathan stayed in Cleveland. Janet was beginning to feel like a single mother emotionally, forming an intense bond with her son that replenished her even as it seemed to take all the energy she had. In Richmond Harry purchased a 4,000-square-foot house surrounded by two acres in the city's af-fluent West End. It was the kind of house that Harry, as general manager of a division, was expected to have. But because of Harry's long hours, Janet found that she and Nathan were often alone together in the big new house. A second pregnancy followed, and Jenna was born.

Harry had his work. Janet had the kids. She and Harry had no life together. Depressed and overweight, Janet felt trapped in the large showplace house. Sometimes she knew Harry didn't come home because he couldn't bear to be there with her. She tried to lose weight and failed, tried to be the corporate wife and hated the role. But motherhood, *that* never asked too much. She and the kids had this language, this space, this emotional place that was all theirs. They made her feel strong. By the time Harry came home most nights, Jenna and Nathan were in the tub, or asleep and dreaming in the aftermath of a story Janet had read them before bed.

Janet didn't know it then, she couldn't, but all the long hours in the showcase house alone with Nathan and Jenna were *her* gestation. Bonding with first her son and then her daughter, entrenched in one of the world's most valuable endeavors, Janet was not merely marking time, she was silently, carefully, unconsciously building the skills and confidence she would later call on as a single mother. In the house alone with her children, she learned to trust herself and to know, despite eternal doubts, how skilled and capable and talented she was. In the rooms of the expensively decorated but soulless house that sometimes made her feel like a madwoman in the attic, Janet was storing up strength upon strength as she functioned as primary caregiver and nurturer, and received as much love as she gave.

But parenthood couldn't change the desperate state of her marriage. Silence, distance, and mistrust prevailed, but still Janet and Harry tried for three years after Jenna's birth to make the marriage work. Harry agreed to marriage counseling as a couple, but stopped attending sessions after three months. Janet stayed in counseling, for in the therapist she had found not only someone to talk to, but someone to listen, someone who was aiding and abetting the process of growth Nathan and Jenna had inspired.

Therapy forced Janet to acknowledge her lack of self-esteem, gave a name to the fears that had plagued her for so long. The therapist suggested she read *Women Who Run with the Wolves,* the bestselling book chronicling many of the most enduring myths of power and struggle and rebirth that could codify women's belief in self. Reading and re-reading, savoring and carrying the book around with her in internal regions of daring and dream, Janet was slowly transformed. Eventually it was she who decided that the marriage had to end, and she asked for a divorce. By then, half a dozen of her friends who lived in the showplace houses around her were divorcing too. "They were there for me, I was there for them, we packed up each other's houses, watched each other's kids. Seeing my friends divorce and go on made me feel that it wouldn't be the end of the world, that I could survive." Janet was stronger than she knew, stronger than she felt. It was she who had known that she had to be a mother no matter what, and that she could be a good mother. She had taken the risk and brought her children to life in a troubled marriage, a marriage where her children were all she had to believe in. Having decided to reclaim her life, Janet went back to school.

In school, she says, "I could use the big words I liked to use without being criticized for being pretentious. I was more myself, I was doing things I was good at." After the divorce, which provided a comfortable settlement and generous child support, Janet moved into a house in a suburban subdivision in Hanover County, Virginia, where she had the contractor build the house the way her grandfather told her a house should be, a square with a staircase in the middle. And everything in the house represents her. She won't bring anything into the house that doesn't reflect her spirit, her soul. By choosing to live in the suburbs, she found that she could regularly call on other stay-at-home or part-time employed mothers in the neighborhood to help with Jenna and Nathan. The community even had a baby-sitting co-op.

Now she was alone and that was scary, for she had never been alone, never taken full unequivocal responsibility for herself. There was always Mom, Dad, and then Harry. But with her children in the new house, which she began to call home, Janet found that the little things mattered most and made it all less frightening. Making papier mâché figures with Nathan and Jenna, eating three meals a day together, every day, all the time, not just eating but sharing each other, being a family. The first night in the new house, she was sorting clothes, filling the washing machine in the hall and talking to the kids, who were in the bathtub, and all of a sudden she felt, *This is right, this is as it should be.* She had been a mother in a comfortable cocoon; now she was mother in the real, no-escape world. And no matter what, she was going to find a way to get for herself and her kids what they needed.

Janet learned new skills, little things other women, other mothers, took for granted. During the holidays she drove the kids home to Ohio alone for the first time. It was a ten-hour drive with the kids. Before, Harry had done all the driving on the holiday trips home. Two hours from home, Janet turned to look at Jenna beside her, saw the pale, drained-of-blood pallor, the frightened look on her face, and instinctively grabbed a nearby paper towel and caught the sickness spewing out of Jenna's choked throat just in time. One hand on the wheel, the other hand holding a paper towel drenched in her daughter's sickness, she didn't know whether to scream or to laugh, but she knew all at once that she could do this, she could go it alone.

Gradually Janet realized she wanted to write, and now she was willing to accept whatever came in the wake of the words. The essay she wrote for my class was included in an anthology that featured well-known writers and was released by a major publisher. This convinced her that "I *have* to write. I didn't always believe I could, but now that I know I can, I damn well better." The essay helped her break through a barrier, move to another level, one that was both more dangerous and more safe. She could never be the same. Writing about her children and herself changed her life. Her ambitions slowly stepped forth. She thought that maybe she'd teach as well as write, and always be the world's best mom, and know that she could do all three; and that even if it wasn't easy, it was important, it was necessary, it was what she had to do. She continued the therapy and felt herself growing every day, just like Nathan, just like Jenna.

There were conversations she now had with herself that no one had ever prepared her to have, dialogues that she shaped alone in the dark, and even driving in the car with the kids—conversations about self-reliance, and trusting what you feel. This is what she wanted Nathan and Jenna to know, how important that was. They saw her doing/being every day, but that wasn't enough. She had to tell them, to talk to them about it. She wanted them to know that she could do anything she set her mind to, and that meant they could too. She was all-purpose—a Brownie leader who learned how to Rollerblade, and a feminist literary critic.

And, more than anything, she wanted Jenna to know that women were as valuable as men. Janet's heart nearly broke the day she caught her daughter smearing chapstick in the small holes inside the knobs attached to the dresser drawers, and heard Jenna respond to her query about why she had done it by saying, childishly, self-effacingly, " 'Cause I'm stupid." The words reminded Janet of all the times before and during her marriage when the worst thing she feared, exactly what she dreaded, happened to her because somewhere deep inside she felt enslaved by the same doubts. She wondered if insecurity was passed through the genes. So she vowed to nudge and talk and push and love Jenna into knowing that she was bright and smart and wonderful and loved. Over and over she told Nathan and Jenna what she had rarely heard: "Be kind to yourself, do what's right for you." Every day she grieved for the marriage she had lost, and she stitched together, with trembling fingers, a solid, grounded, sure sense of herself and what she could do. She was taking baby steps toward loving and trusting herself, and she never stopped taking the steps, even if she sometimes tripped and fell.

Janet studies Zen and meditates, weaves the wisdom of sages into her life and the lives of her children. She's still in therapy, and thinks of it as a kind of meditation. Her therapist is her friend now, not a crutch. Now she can see how her own insecurity, her own doubts, made her a victim in her marriage. All the silence, all the anguish, wasn't only Harry's fault. She now knows there are ways in which she failed him too.

Now, for the sake of the children, for the sake of themselves, she and Harry build bridges they couldn't before. Nathan and Jenna, as children of divorce, are marked, and some would say irreparably crippled, but Janet is teaching them to find meaning and salvation in the suffering that, at their tender ages, they endure.

Harry flies down every three weeks from Chicago, where he now lives, and spends the weekend with the children in a hotel. The divorce settlement was generous enough to allow Janet not to work if she chose, but she considers the generosity nothing more than what the children and she as their mother deserve. She is still the one on call twenty-four/seven to wipe bloody noses and answer a thousand questions. Sometimes she thinks about the future and wonders if she will marry again. But for now she feels too fragile, has too much work to do on herself and her spirit, and is enjoying getting to know the woman she is too much to want to have a relationship with a man, to fall in love. One day. But not now.

Over her desk, the desk where she writes every day, Janet has placed the words of psychologist Carl Jung:

Nothing has a stronger influence psychologically on their environment and especially on their children, than the unlived lives of parents.

Janet's not a white-bread girl anymore. If she were asked, she'd say she was something thick and pungent like pumpernickel, a bread that fills you up and that tastes like the bread of life. She has what she wanted and feared and got and chose: a reality, a something to struggle against so that tension would keep making her over every day. She had thought life was a lesson, something like school, but it's more like writing, like mothering—a chance simply to re-create herself every day. She resides in the center of her own world, no longer on the margins. And it doesn't have to be a perfect fit, often it's more than she can bear, but having to be there for Nathan and Jenna makes her present-and-accounted-for to herself too. Some days the fount dries up, other times it gushes, but at least now she knows the spring is there. All she had to do to turn it on was believe. And she must have been able to believe long before the children. Maybe they were always inside her, and were the seeds of belief just waiting to come out so *she* could be born.

"My kids have taught me that the most important thing in life is family. I didn't feel that way growing up. I now have the family life I wanted as a child."

FIVE WEEKS AFTER her first daughter, Nikki, was born, Yolanda English's husband, Kevin, left her. He gathered and removed his clothes from the parking lot of their apartment complex, where she had thrown them from their window in angry retaliation, then returned twice to drive off with both their cars. Kevin left her—because, she says, "he had decided he didn't want to be married anymore"—and Yolanda sat in her apartment in tears, clinging to the daughter that in time would become a comfort and a motivation to rebuild her life.

Marooned in the apartment with a new baby during one of the hottest Maryland summers on record, with no access to the bank account that had been opened in Kevin's name only, Yolanda couldn't even walk to the nearby grocery store because she feared the effect of the heat on Nikki. She found a way through the night, and the next day, and the days that followed, largely because, in the midst of this crisis, Yolanda's fellow employees rallied around her. The managers of Copeland Company, where she was a commission-only salesperson of tax annuities, chipped in to buy her a twelve-hundred-dollar Toyota Corolla so she could have the mobility she needed to make sales. Every Friday, for several weeks, an anonymous fellow employee left a hundred-dollar bill in her mailbox. When she was close to being evicted from her apartment, a friend referred Yolanda to a recently divorced teacher who had a vacant room in her house she was willing to rent. When the three-hundred-dollar rent was more than Yolanda could handle, the friend told her to simply take the money and save it for an apartment. A year later, Yolanda bounced back and was recognized as one of the top fifteen salespeople nationally for Copeland, and was rewarded with a trip to La Costa, California.

Resilience, hard work, the love of her child—mostly the love of her child, Yolanda will tell you—is what saved her. "I used to run up the stairs to get Nikki each day at the baby-sitter's. I mean I ached to see her at the end of the day. I loved being a mother."

But being a mother was a challenge for this young single woman employed in sales, one of the most demanding professions. She had always been competitive, loved educating people and helping them to plan for the future. Working on commission was like walking a high wire with no safety net, for sales is a profession full of risks and no guarantees; but Yolanda saw all that as the impetus to put her innate drive and love of challenges in action. Her family in New York thought she was crazy—a single mother working straight commission—but by the time Nikki was two, Yolanda was making nearly forty thousand dollars a year, more than anyone in her family.

Born in Harlem, one of four children raised in the Jefferson Projects to a striving working-class family, Yolanda was the middle child, a bright, studious achiever at Our Lady Queen of Angels, the Catholic school that sat right in the middle of the projects. Of her youth in Harlem in the early sixties she says, "My life was sheltered, I never saw drugs, or much crime. The streets and the neighborhood were pretty safe." But conflicts with her stepfather, and the lack of space in the cramped two-bedroom apartment, drove Yolanda to spend much of her time away from home. When she left in the morning for school, often Yolanda wouldn't return until late in the evening, doing her homework at a friend's house. Her memories of childhood center more around time spent with girlfriends on 115th Street and Amsterdam Avenue than around time shared with her mother, stepfather, and siblings. It was at Wilberforce University, the country's first black college, located in Wilberforce, Ohio, that Yolanda says she grew in confidence and purpose. She was president of her sorority, the AKAs, president of the honor society, and a student representative for the board of trustees, all while majoring in finance. She won the John F. Morning Award for outstanding senior business major. And at the business school Yolanda was exposed to some of the country's most prominent black businessmen.

But after graduation, the transition to the world of work was rocky. After a disastrous first job as an accountant with a firm in Canton, Ohio, that made alloy steel and roller bearings (an experience that led her to file a discrimination suit), Yolanda realized that she wanted to work in sales because she liked working directly with people. She was also drawn to the commission aspect of sales because she wanted a salary that recognized and rewarded her drive and ambition.

In the aftermath of her brief marriage to Kevin and the difficult separation and divorce, Yolanda found herself so busy rebuilding her life, and making a present and a future for Nikki, that she had little time for depression. Her daughter seemed wise beyond her years and offered Yolanda, during the separation and divorce, a steady comfort she could never have predicted or expected from a child.

With the divorce behind her, Yolanda switched from selling tax annuities to selling pharmaceuticals. "I wasn't growing as a salesperson. I needed more of a challenge, and when the recession hit, teachers simply weren't investing." Through a friend, Yolanda found out about the lucrative job of selling pharmaceuticals, a job in which she would be provided with a car and an expense account, something she lacked as a commission-only salesperson of tax annuities. When she talked to corporate headhunters, she was told she'd never be hired because she didn't have a background in medicine. But for Yolanda the warnings had an unintended effect. "If you tell me I'll never do something, that just makes me work harder to achieve it."

On her own, through her network of contacts in the business, Yolanda finally landed an interview with a pharmaceuticals firm. The night of her second interview, Yolanda settled Nikki in the living room with a Barney video and talked to the manager of the firm on her bedroom phone. During the interview, which was going almost perfectly, convincing Yolanda that the job was virtually hers, Nikki came into the bedroom and asked for a cookie. Flustered, Yolanda waved Nikki away, telling her she'd be off the phone soon. Moments later the manager abruptly ended the call. She wasn't hired, and Yolanda found out later that she was being interviewed to replace a woman who had quit because of the demands of motherhood. She didn't get the job but was hired a week later by Ciba-Geigy, one of the country's major pharmaceutical companies. Shortly after beginning the job Yolanda got pregnant, and says simply, "As a Christian, I didn't believe in abortion.

"All my friends thought I was crazy. They couldn't understand my decision. But I felt like, having survived what I'd gone through with Kevin, I had proven how strong I was. But it was hard. The baby's father, who was separated from his wife, begged me to have an abortion; then, when he knew I wouldn't, he kept coming in and out of my life making and breaking promises, saying he'd always be there, then not calling for weeks, making my life miserable. I cried for seven months. I was determined to have my baby but I was still scared. My daughter Nikki was my best friend through it all. One night I was crying and she came to me with a tissue and told me, 'Jesus loves you and so do I.' At three years old she was my rock; her smile, her love, she gave me so much joy through both the crisis with Kevin and my pregnancy with Nia."

The pregnancy with Nia was a long dark night of the soul. Yolanda had made the decision to keep this child, knew that she had enough strength and enough love, and the only real challenge was to make more money. But the pregnancy was difficult, filled with emotional turmoil, because of the doubt of friends. When she told one friend that she was pregnant, the woman immediately asked, "So when are you having the abortion?" But Yolanda felt that saying yes to Nia was saying yes to herself. She knew what nobody else did—that she could do this, be mother to another child, and she could do it alone. And she didn't care if anyone understood.

The decision to give birth to Nia forced Yolanda into one of the most challenging moments of clarification in her life up to then. She was single and pregnant. Her friends saw the child she carried as a mistake that could be fixed. But what the skeptical, well-meaning friends didn't know was that she was *filled* with child. And she was also full of love.

It was the worst possible time, for she had just started the job at Ciba-Geigy. Sure it mattered to her what people thought. But what mattered more was what *she* felt. Very few people saw the decision to keep the baby as courageous. Another child would be an inconvenience. Wasn't it hard enough already with Nikki? Was she a fool or did she think she was a saint? Some of her friends phrased their discomfort with her decision in words as blunt and cruel. Yolanda found it nearly impossible to explain, even to her closest friends, what it had meant to her to be Nikki's mother, her *single* mother. This was love, what she and Nikki had. Her daughter had been there for her with an innocent, open, giving spirit that replenished and saved her. Her dreams, her ambitions, everything she was and hoped for and wanted was bigger, more complex, bolder now because of her child. She was scared, but somehow deep inside knew that there was really nothing to fear.

It was the hardest decision she'd ever made, and she cried every day even after making it. Not out of regret. But because even the right decision was hard. Saying yes rather than no made her feel lonelier than she had ever felt. It didn't matter that no one understood. But because they didn't, she felt isolated from the support of women she still respected and loved.

Looking back, Yolanda is convinced that the turmoil of those nine months affected Nia. "I'm convinced she felt my pain, all I was going through, maybe she could even hear my tears, because she is very clingy and insecure." The church Yolanda attended refused to baptize Nia during the regular Sunday service because Yolanda wasn't married. Yolanda remembers, "They said they'd do it during the week in a side chapel."

When Nia was born, Yolanda now had not just another baby, but a different kind of family. The girlfriends who had acted as Nikki's surrogate family now stepped in to provide support and assistance for Nia. Yolanda still felt herself on call twenty-four/seven but she worked even harder, switching after a few years to a new area of sales— selling surgical implants to surgeons, a job that requires that she travel around the country as many as five days a month for training meetings. This being away from Nikki and Nia so much is the downside of the job she loves. Sometimes she takes the girls with her. And she says, "I miss them so much when I'm gone. I really realize what I have waiting for me when I come home."

And in the home that Yolanda has made with her daughters, she keeps learning and the girls keep teaching her how to be their mother, how to give them what they need. Kevin spends time with Nikki regularly, and because Nia's father plays no role in her life, Kevin includes Nia in excursions and time shared with Nikki. But Nia craves male attention, is needy and clingy, and so Yolanda has asked a friend to act as Nia's godfather, as Nia's surrogate dad.

When she looks at her life now, Yolanda concludes, "The home I have now with my children is a peaceful home. My daughters know they are loved and they know how to express love." This is the home she wanted as a child. Everything in her life has ultimately, even after all the pain, been about progress. Everyone told her another child would ruin her life, but the birth of Nia only expanded it. Yolanda had envisioned herself, when she was a student at Wilberforce, as a dedicated career woman. Her job promotions, salary, these would be the most important things. But family turned out to be the best and most important reality of all. She and Nikki and Nia are a family. No one can tell her they aren't.

Still, her prayer is to give herself and the girls even more. She would like someone to love. If she could give the girls anything right now, it would be that, the gift of seeing her loved and loving a man. But she's not waiting, not putting her life or their lives on hold. There's too much to do right now. There's too much love she already has that she doesn't want to miss.

"I was so busy paying the bills and trying to get from one day to the next, I had stopped paying attention to my kids. I had to get refocused. I had to pay attention."

To create a nurturing, positive family, Michelle Bachteler had to leave her husband. Before she could take responsibility for the life she wanted to make, she had to stop drinking. When she did both, Michelle says she finally became a mother, in the most total and meaningful sense, to her three children.

There were always two Michelles; in fact, maybe three. Her long dark hair, olive-toned complexion, full lips, deep-set eyes, and languid carriage always perplexed and intrigued. This Italian girl born in Hartford, Connecticut, was sometimes mistaken for a Hispanic. Some wondered if she was half black. Because her looks implied a kind of exoticism that men found appealing, people thought she knew more, had done more, possessed more wisdom and experience than she really did. Then there was the young woman behind the outer shell: shy, quiet, unsure, needy. This alter ego wanted to be the confident, in-control person everyone assumed she was.

This dreamy tomboy who loved to read, the only girl of four children, left home at sixteen. Her parents had moved from Connecticut to settle in Bowie, Maryland, when Michelle was thirteen. During her teenage years, her parents, once Catholic, joined the Church of the Nazarene, a strict religious sect that prohibited drinking, smoking, wearing makeup, dating, watching television, reading newspapers; and mandated church attendance three days a week.

At sixteen, Michelle, who already looked twenty-one, was drinking and sneaking out of the house at night to be with her boyfriend. She drank and smoked because her friends did, and the two activities made her feel adult, helped her relax. When she felt the buzz and the smooth, easy indifference the alcohol induced, she could talk easily, joke as expertly as her friends. She wasn't Michelle anymore. She was somebody else.

Michelle felt that her mother had declared war on her, armed with the rules and requirements of the family's new faith. Everything that made her feel alive, her mother saw as a symbol of death and future damnation. They argued constantly over who she went out with, the boys who called her on the phone. Often Michelle came home after school to find her closets and drawers open, her belongings out of place, and she knew instinctively that her mother had been reading her diary. One afternoon she found her clothes amassed in a wild heap on her bed, cut up into shreds because her mother said they made her look cheap, like an instrument of the devil.

Michelle's mother also accused her father of spoiling and favoring Michelle because she was the only girl. Her brothers were afraid to stand up for her, and, under siege and increasingly isolated, Michelle moved out when her mother told her she had to leave if she refused to live by her rules. She missed her senior year of high school and stayed with her boyfriend's family in Connecticut, then the next year came back to Bowie and lived with family friends while completing her final year at Bowie High.

Determined and eager to prove her independence, Michelle entered Prince Georges Community College to study prelaw, then enrolled in a local school for paralegals that offered a degree. While in college, her looks and personality easily got her jobs as a cocktail waitress, or bartender at the Marriott or Sheraton hotels in the area.

She was on her own, independent, and everyone who looked at her thought she was a woman, but she felt like a little girl inside. She worked hard, made good grades, and got her paralegal degree. It was important, she knew even then, to prove that she was smart, that there was more to her than how she looked. She had her own apartment in College Park and was working in law firms in the area. She went out regularly at night to drink and party with her friends.

They went to rock and roll clubs, semidark places lit by neon lights, places with half a dozen bars inside and music so loud it pounded everything you feared into oblivion, places with names like Hammerjack's and Hurricane. It was at Hammerjack's that Michelle met Russell. He was a drummer in his own band and he was everything she wasn't—funny, charismatic, and outgoing. Everyone wanted to be around him. Russell always had a story that broke everyone up, and he looked like the kind of guy who was his own man.

Like virtually all the other women in their group, Michelle was attracted to him. And he wanted her. She was twenty-one, a "career girl," and everyone thought she was in control of her life. Sometimes, especially when she was at work or with her friends, she felt like she was. It was only when she was alone that she knew what nobody else did. But Russell, for a while, made all that doubt disappear.

They started dating, and six months later Michelle was pregnant. She had already had one abortion and had sworn never to do it again, so for her there was no choice but to have the baby, a decision Michelle stuck to even after she drove to Baltimore one morning to see Russell and found him in bed with another woman. She kept the baby even though already the turbulent outline of their future had etched itself in stone. Arguments, sometimes physical fights, had become their primary mode of communication. During her pregnancy they broke up. Michelle had thought she was independent but soon realized she needed help. After the baby was born, a boy she named Jason, Michelle moved in with Russell's mother. It was easier living with her than with her own disapproving parents. A year later, she and Russell reconciled and moved into their own apartment. Then Christine was born.

They married but weren't really a family. Russell tried to be a father to Jason and Christine, but his own father hadn't provided a model of fatherhood for him, and he struggled. Russell sometimes felt as if he'd had to raise himself while his mother was away working as a truck driver and his father was out drinking. He had become a father by accident, and he knew he wasn't up to facing the task. He hated himself for his inability to give Jason and Christine what he had lacked, and he was angry with Michelle for wanting the children, because their existence, he felt, merely revealed his inadequacy.

The small apartment was the stage for their mutual passion, desire, and weakness. When times were good, they'd leave the children with friends or relatives and hit the bars, where Michelle felt it was like the beginning, and like maybe she and Russell could recapture what had made them want each other. But they always had to go home, where they faced the stack of bills somebody (usually Michelle) had to pay, home, where Jason and Christine witnessed the fights and heard the arguments over money, other women, how to raise the children. After a while even the numbness that crept up on her in the bars didn't provide relief. The birth of a third child, Brittany, ended any illusion that they could make it, and a year after Brittany's birth Michelle and Russell separated.

Michelle moved into her own place and stopped drinking. She had grown tired of the hangovers, of feeling sick the morning after another binge. Alone in her own place with her children, Michelle realized that the most important choices she had made in her adult life had been made "under the influence." The confidence the alcohol gave her was an illusion. When she stopped drinking, a process that required six months, she never drank again. Then the depression hit her. She felt like she had no personality; but finally she could see her children with unclouded vision, and she could see what they had been denied.

Michelle had been running away ever since she could remember, first from home, then from her mother, but ultimately and always from herself. She changed jobs a lot, sought out the bars because they provided distraction and excitement. Even the relationship with Russell was an escape, for her efforts to hold on to him, to please him, sidetracked her from thinking about herself, about who she was and wanted to be besides his wife.

On her own with the children, Michelle finally had to stop running. Extricating herself from the marriage to Russell, however, was as difficult as their union had been. The arguments continued, this time on the phone, but there were also surprise pop visits by Russell that turned into ugly skirmishes. He wanted her back. She refused to return. In retaliation, Russell held back child support. Even after the divorce, resisting court orders, he simply wouldn't pay. In the midst of this, Michelle had the twin jobs of discovering herself anew and protecting and providing for the children, who became her allies. Jason was energetic, outgoing, truly Russell's son; Christine was eager to please, nurturing; and Brittany was independent, unpredictable.

Michelle's father had always played an active role in the children's lives, and to offset Russell's absence he spent even more time with his grandchildren. She asked her brothers to do the same and they did. Soon Michelle felt the stirrings of a yearning to know and complete herself as well. Through a friend, she heard about a women's support group in her area. The women met to talk about their lives and to give each other support, but too often it seemed to Michelle that the subject of men dominated the conversation. Michelle had joined to find a space to talk about herself. Soon she stopped going.

She joined a Unity Church in Bowie, drawn by its nondoctrinaire religious principles that emphasized her own spiritual power. For the first time in her adult life she was choosing her own circles of support, friendships, and community. Her life with Russell, when she looked back on it, seemed so small, so stifling, she wondered how she had survived it. In the church, she made new friends and found a psychological grounding the children needed.

But nine-year-old Jason had started setting fires, his grades had plummeted and he had joined a group of boys at school who were chronically in trouble. A year earlier Michael, the brother Michelle and the children were closest to, had died of AIDS. Michelle was convinced that Jason's anger was directed at his absent father and was a sign of his grief over losing his favorite uncle. Jason needed close supervision, more of her time.

One of the lawyers at the firm she worked for had been sexually harassing her. The firm offered Michelle several months severance pay not to sue. She decided to accept their offer and seize the opportunity to have time during the day for Jason. She found a night job word-processing for another law firm three nights a week, while a family member watched the kids. She worked with Jason's teachers to monitor him closely. His grades and behavior improved. She had lost a job but found a new way to be present for the children and herself.

Michelle was learning to balance her life and to respond creatively to the changes and challenges that never stopped coming. She rented out a room in her house and began baby-sitting children in the neighborhood to supplement her part-time salary, anything to maintain the kind of life she had now, one that enabled her to be at home when the children got out of school, to spend more time with them, and to develop herself, tend to her own needs and dreams as well.

To conquer the shyness that had always plagued her, Michelle joined Toastmasters, a national organization that helps people develop the skill of public speaking. She was finding herself and her voice. She wasn't exactly sure of everything she wanted to say, but she knew she wanted the world to hear it. Russell was changing too, finally agreeing to pay the long-overdue child support and visiting the children once a week.

Michelle's favorite word these days is *power,* a word that she likes the sound of, the implications of, and tries, with everything she does, to weave into her life. She thinks a lot about her power as a woman, her power as a mother, the strength her children have given her, and what she has given them. Brittany, Jason, and Christine, she will tell you, halted her careening, headlong journey to nowhere, focused her, and helped her find a path larger and more promising than she might have imagined without them.

IN MY FATHER'S HOUSE

The emotional resilience and everyday courage that allow single mothers to create healthy homes and lives for their children does not erase the impact of the absent father. Whether he is a weekend dad or a father never or rarely seen, the man who is ex-husband or former lover occupies a crucial place in the home of single mother and child. Ask your child to tell you her secret wish, his most frequent dream, and it will be for a father at the dinner table, a dad to help with homework. Think of the person who can inspire the most intense mixture of anguish and love, and it may be your children's father. The legacy of the absent father extends its reach into and shapes expectations, becomes the shadow the child longs to hold. The absent father paces the rooms of the home that the single mother and child inhabit, an unacknowledged yet powerful ghost.

When criticizing your child, how often do you conclude that he is "just like your father"? Can you recall the last time you praised your child and attributed a positive characteristic to the father who isn't around? Physically absent but emotionally pervasive, the absent father is there, every step of the way, with mother and child; his spirit, and the interpretation of what and who he is, is stoking either love or bitterness, acceptance or mistrust.

Striving for wholeness and healing of self is the "soul" foundation of the single mother's life, and it inevitably must lead to forging, whenever possible, bonds of trust and love with the father of her children. To act otherwise is to unfairly cast us and our children outside the realm of our children's father's love. This journey is fraught with even more fear and doubt than the task of engaging the self. For, like manic bookkeepers, we store on the ledger of our hearts and minds every past and present hurt. My son was the source of the greatest conflict in the form of a custody battle—in my separation and divorce from my first husband. But Michael was, a decade later, the inspiration for my move to reconcile with my former husband. My love for my son was so deep that it emboldened me to do what I swore I never would—forgive and accept his father as the man he was. Every day that I waged war in my mind on my son's father, there was no rest or peace for me or my son.

Everything I said to my son was a lie as long as I failed to find the courage in myself to move past knee-jerk anger into a zone of renewal and healing.

A mother's love for her children has traditionally been assumed to be deeper, more all-encompassing than a father's. The legal, cultural, and social eminence of a mother in the life of her child often makes the real, very deep emotions that fathers feel for their children seem peripheral. But our children are the children of mothers *and* fathers. Any mother who consciously or unconsciously weakens the bonds between father and child denies her child a part of himself.

The father's "house" is constructed by father, mother, and child, and it is filled with rooms of both darkness and light, and condemned spaces marked by neglect. But it is a house that, because it is built by mother, father, and child, belongs to all and can be redesigned at any and at every moment. Every child in a single-parent home deserves a mother at peace with herself and her child's father. Every child of a single parent deserves the opportunity to love and make peace with his father.

Fathers link their children to a profound sense of themselves. What our children need most from their fathers is attention and emotional commitment. Michael Lindsey says that, growing up in Fairfax Village, watching his friends on Fort Davis Street whose fathers lived at home, he saw that, "All those dads did was work. I hardly ever saw them spend time with their kids. They had fathers in the home. But sometimes it didn't seem like they had much more than me." In the years immediately following Charlotte and Clarence's separation and divorce, the relationship between Clarence Lindsey and his sons was marked by regular visits and consistent attention. After he remarried, however, and assumed the role of stepfather to his new wife's children, Michael and Charlotte say that the time spent with his sons became less consistent, and as a result the boys felt rejected, cast aside. The primary emotional burden of helping her sons hold on to their love for their father, even as they felt the outward signs of that love waning, was borne by Charlotte, a burden made heavier by the feeling that in sense she was mother to two entirely different sets of children.

The oldest sons, Wesley and Gerald, had known Clarence Lindsey as an active presence in their lives. Ronald was five when the separation occurred. Michael was three, and David was born in the midst of the breakup. These younger sons had looser bonds with their father. And inevitably it fell on Charlotte to help her sons navigate their way through the turmoil of their feelings about their father, a job that was difficult and often thankless and that required her sometimes to bury her own anguish; but she says, "I told them always to respect him and to honor him as their father."

It was Ronald, the middle son, whose anguish was most dramatically evident. He frequently got into trouble in school, seemed always to be involved in fights, and once hid his report card for six months without showing it to Charlotte, because of poor grades. When Charlotte punished him for hiding his report card, he wrote her a letter trying to explain the source of his anguish and actions, telling her that she didn't know what it was like to grow up without a father. But with characteristic bluntness and confidence, Charlotte told Ronald, "No, I don't know what it's like growing up without a father, but I'm telling you, you don't have to be like you are because you don't have a father. You find a father image at church. Somebody that you can relate to, somebody that you can talk to, you find that person at church."

Ultimately Ronald developed a strong relationship with a coach at school. The pastor of her church often helped Charlotte guide her sons, gave advice and counseling. "If anything happened to my boys, I don't care what it was, I sought my pastor's advice," she told me.

Of Charlotte's three youngest sons, Michael is the one who has most consistently sought to sustain a relationship with his father. He has been bridge builder and peacemaker between his father and the sons he left behind. Their relationship has been, over the years, an enduring work-in-progress, marked by constantly shifting levels of intimacy.

When the article in the *Washington Post* appeared, Clarence Lindsey was stung by the article's implication that he had done little or nothing for his children and that he had played no role in their lives. Perception is reality. Clarence Lindsey saw an article that praised the strength of his former wife and his sons as a family that had made it against the odds. He saw an article that did not mention his child support payments or the time he had spent with his sons. What he saw was, he felt, a distortion and, he must have felt, an injustice. But what his sons perceived was a father who they felt had remarried and then de-escalated his role in their lives.

The chasm between these two perceptions has inflicted pain on father and sons. Michael, during the months of our interviews, spoke of the counseling he was receiving to help him deal with a number of personal issues, some of which sprang from his relationship with his father. During one conversation, I could hear the pain and yearning in his voice as he told me that he had been reaching out to his father again, trying to sustain and forge communication.

I told Michael that he must remember all the things his father *had* given him. Clarence Lindsey is a minister and clearly Michael, too, is "called." The law, politics, social work, all beckoned to Michael as possible career paths because each one, he thought, offered the opportunity to "make a difference." It became obvious to me that he *would* make sense of his life because he was the son of both his mother and his father. From both his parents he had inherited drive, intelligence, the will to succeed. Both Charlotte Carter and Clarence Lindsey had undergone major and riveting personal transformations that led them to the church, his father to lead one and his mother to become a pillar of another.

I urged Michael to tell his father that he was grateful to him for all that he *had* given him, and to forgive him for all that he felt he had not. "I really *do* love my father," he insisted near the end of our conversation, with the plaintive conviction I had come to expect from him. "We've worked hard to have a relationship and sometimes it's been there. Sometimes it hasn't. But I *do* love him."

For all the questioning and anguish, the journeying into his own soul and the souls of others, that has inspired Michael, he could not have embarked on such a dangerous, potentially treacherous path if he were not convinced of his father's love. But over the years Michael found other fathers in coaches, deacons, professors, all of whom treated him like a son. At Morehouse, in Professor Larry Crawford, a sociology professor, Michael found a mentor and intellectual father figure. The courses in African American sociology and a class on "The Black Male Experience" that Crawford taught helped Michael sort out the reasons for his anger. In his relationship with Crawford, he found a male with whom he could share his feelings and ideas, and who modeled the power of the intellect and teaching. While at Howard, Dr. Lawrence Gary encouraged Michael to research and write about the sociology of black males raised in single-parent homes. But in the end none of those men could tell him who he was, as his own father could.

Michael became a man by protecting the love he felt for his father, by stoking it like a pilot light in his heart. Even at war with, at distance from, his father, he unconsciously modeled himself after Clarence Lindsey, choosing to connect himself to his father even when it may have felt as if they were far apart. Clarence Lindsey's influence on his sons was real, vital, potent. Each son gained from him a different legacy, according to their individual personalities. Each son saw Clarence Lindsey through his own prism of needs and desire, his own private heaven and hell. Charlotte Carter never maligned the father of her sons. Instead she bravely and wisely surrounded her sons with surrogate fathers who could do what she could not: provide the focal point for the necessary separation of her sons' identities from hers.

Clarence Lindsey was not there, but he was never forgotten. Michael and his father failed, fought, and then reached out, tentatively, begrudgingly, proudly, passionately. Even as the sons David and Ronald swore never to forgive their father, never to reach out, they made the vow because of the depth of the love they felt, and felt they had been denied. Like Michael, in the end they came home to the man they would have to acknowledge and forgive in order to know themselves. During the months of my interviews with Charlotte and Michael, Michael was accepted into the doctoral program in social work at the University of Pittsburgh. Clarence Lindsey, in a grand gesture of pride, solidarity, and acceptance, then began the process of making amends to his sons by seeking to forge bonds of intimacy, with a courage Michael says his father admitted he'd lacked before.

But within months the old habits of distance resurfaced, and Clarence Lindsey withdrew from his sons once again.

In his sociological research, Michael is finding meaning in his private suffering while excavating the suffering of other men. The thesis he wrote was as much autobiography as clinical analysis.

How will my own Michael shape his suffering, what will he shape from the debris left in his life by his absent and distant father? Will the legacy of that absence cripple him or provide a hurdle for him to soar over into an entirely new space? Will that legacy be a mountain he will climb and stand astride, after the journey, proud and unashamed of the bruises it took to get there?

When I asked my son who the men were who had most positively influenced him, he spoke of a man whom I had once thought I would marry. Michael said he learned from him the importance of discipline and how it felt to be nurtured by a man. He also cited the director of a male youth mentoring program whom he remembers for instilling confidence in the boys in his charge; he cited a basketball coach at his boarding school, who had acted as buddy and confidante to him, a youngster far from home; he named his father's brother, who had called him regularly at boarding school and whose enthusiastic love and concern filled the space his father's emotional absence had carved; and he cited my husband, Joe, "because he's been in our life so long."

This tapestry of male influence is testimony to the ability of our children to seek, to find, and to choose their role models. My son was drawn to men whose ability to offer emotional nurturance and to push him to become his best self would be what he would remember. It did not matter that he sometimes failed to meet the high standards these men's concern for him imposed. What he took from his relationships with them was the admonition to love himself and the ability to see that charge through. My Michael has never really lived with or known his father as supporter, guide, and model. Instead he claimed other men as fathers, men of whom he could speak with conviction and an affectionate gleam in his eye. I could not ask more than this, given the history my son and I share. I only wish for him more fathers along the way, who like the others will care for him almost as much as I do. I only wish that he will in the end know how to father himself.

Conventional wisdom asserts that the father-absent home takes its greatest toll on male children. In the African American community the psychological devastation of such homes finds its most dramatic expression in the shockingly high number of black males who are incarcerated. Even factoring in the impact of a racist "justice system," poverty, and the naturally treacherous path that males walk into adulthood, clearly the absence of fathers as moral guides plays a role in the lopsided statistics on black male incarceration. Still, the walking wounded black male victims of father-absent homes who are productive citizens surely out-number the males who act out against their community, and through their transgressions express their anguish.

But the daughters suffer too, for young girls learn how to be women and adults in the most complete way not only from their mothers but from the men who nurture them. Every woman is engaged in a struggle to accept or renounce what her father has left behind. The way in which a father loves or does not love the mother of his daughter or son provides his child with their first lessons in sexual/romantic love.

In homes where the psychological inheritance of an absent father is not addressed, the worst-case scenarios can result. Girls can become highly sexual as they mature, searching for father figures in each man they think they love. Looking for tenderness, these young women can only offer and find sex. In families where the father left abruptly, the female child often chooses emotionally unavailable men who cannot or do not create bonds of intimacy. Absence is the only thing the girl may know in terms of men, and so she will seek an emotionally absent partner. In families where the father has never been present, a woman may search for an idealized father figure in her lovers; and, once married, find that because of the depth of her emotional deprivation, her mate can never make up for the absent father.

The most common dynamic in homes where these issues

are not addressed occurs when the mother inflicts her anger and anguish over past hurts onto her children. Anger becomes the gift that keeps on giving. The mother needs her daughter to help her shoulder the burden of pain inflicted by the father. But the daughter, in order to grow into emotional health, must at some point throw off this legacy or it will undermine and possibly destroy her attempts to love herself or men.

For Claudia Booker, the legacy of her unfinished business with her father echoed into the realm of the relationship with Azulai. Claudia told me, "I saw my father in the summer when I was five and six, then again when I was eleven and twelve, so there were years when I never saw him or heard from him. My mother bought cards and gifts for me on my birthday and at Christmas, and put his name on them and told me he sent them. After a while, as I got older, I could tell it was her handwriting.

"My father couldn't really handle the emotional weight of intimacy, and our relationship was pretty much one of him making promises he didn't keep and me yearning for him to love me. And he was pretty much the same kind of grandfather. When Azulai and I would invite my father to dinner, more times than I want to remember he wouldn't show up and he wouldn't even call. We'd take him gifts on Father's Day, planning to spend the whole day with him, and he'd suggest that we leave after half an hour. One Christmas I had planned to take Azulai to New York City so she could see the Christmas tree at Rockefeller Center, skate in the rink there and have a real New York Christmas. I wanted my father to join us to be part of it. The day before we were to leave, he called and said, 'I just don't feel ready to do this yet.' He broke my heart as a kid, and then he broke Azulai's."

Yet it was Clifford Booker's terminal battle with cancer that tested Claudia's loyalty, love, and faith, and provided, she says, the most important experience that she and her daughter have gone through together. "He went into the hospital for plastic surgery, and in doing the checkup a spot was discovered on his lung. He had lung cancer. It was a swift, tortured, descent. My father died three weeks after the diagnosis. Although he had never really been there much for me, as he was dying he asked me to be there for him, to hold the family together; to be the strong one, a role I knew pretty well how to play. Azulai told me that she simply didn't want to go to the hospital to see him, to stand by him during the days he was dying. She had seen other friends and family members die, so I knew it wasn't that. But she couldn't understand how I could be there for him, how I could spend days by his bedside when he had been so irresponsible. She was pretty angry with him. I told her he was my father and I had no other choice. In all honesty I was hoping that somehow on his deathbed, before it was all over, my father would of course say something to me, ask me to forgive him, give me the love that I'd never felt from him before. That was my agenda. And in my father's hospital room, my father was holding my hand so tight his nails were digging into my palms and almost drawing blood as he struggled to breathe. And yet his last words to me were not ones of love, but he looked at me and told me, 'Claudia, you were always too smart for your own good.'

"His words felt like a cold knife in my heart, but in the aftermath, in the months that passed, I learned that I was finally free; and I don't blame myself anymore, I don't feel anymore that the way he treated me means I deserved to be treated that way. Azulai watched me forgive my father and struggle with the aftermath of his death, and that's been important for her to see. If I hadn't stood by his bedside I would have taught her the wrong lesson, and I wouldn't have gained closure." Clearly Claudia's father recognized her strength and did love her, for he made her executor of his estate and left each of his children generous financial gifts.

To the experience of single parenthood Claudia brought the strength of her mother and all the surrogate mothers she had known, as well as the unfinished business of the emotional neglect inflicted by her father. But clearly the confidence and assurance she gained from her mother and female relatives gave her the power to steadfastly meet her father's irresponsibility and indifference with love. Every time she gave her father another chance to love her right this time, she set an example for Azulai of spiritual maturity. Azulai saw patience, forgiveness, and love of father modeled by the very vulnerable mother she had thought was so strong. She saw that her mother's love for her father was unquenchable, and very deep.

In believing in her father's love, yearning for it and honoring her father up to the end, Claudia gave her daughter a tangible, usable image of forgiveness, patience, loyalty, and love. Azulai, although unable to understand all that she saw, nevertheless learned that real love is unconditional. Azulai also witnessed her grandfather's need for the daughter he could rarely find a way to embrace. This is the story—one of death and dying and legacies and love songs never sung by a father terrified to sing in those keys—that Claudia says is the most important one that she and her daughter have constructed together. In the aftermath of her father's death, Claudia says, "I now really understand unconditional love. I am the conduit of it. It was passed to me. I pass it on to Azulai."

In her search for the right man to father her child, and in her determination to make Clifford Booker *be* a father, Claudia's wounds shaped the style and meaning of her love for the child she so bravely brought into her life. Her father's death, at long last, propelled her into a place of healing. In those three weeks that were a dying and a living, a clinging to life, an argument with it, Claudia was tested; and she stumbled to a kind of triumph. There was no other place for her to be than by her father's side, with or without Azulai. The courage she called on to heed her father's wish that she once again be the good daughter, will undoubtedly resonate with Azulai, just as her own mother's choices echo inside Claudia. Still, she had never plunged so deep, where all is blessedly still and so peaceful and terrifying at the same time.

Her father's death, because of her response to it, gave Claudia a new way to imagine living and defining herself. Claudia will always be Clifford Booker's daughter, and the daughter of the women in the house on Superior Avenue. Azulai will always be her child. Standing before her daughter, Claudia said yes to everything—the beauty and the terror. One day Azulai will know how to speak, because her mother did. She will sing love on key in a clear, lilting voice that Claudia will hear wherever she is.

∞

THIS BATTLE OVER the remains of a tumultuous father-love is one that Eunice Ogletree is waging. A nurse at a suburban hospital outside Washington, D.C., Eunice is a tall, imposing woman whose demeanor immediately asserts her presence, and whose voice and apparent compassion put one at ease.

Over dinner in a downtown restaurant Eunice told me the story of her mother, her father, and herself. Eunice and her older sister were raised by their schoolteacher mother in Suitland, Maryland. When asked to describe her father, Eunice said, "He was kind of missing in action."

Her parents separated when Eunice was an infant and her sister was six, and she says that she has seen her father maybe seven or eight times since he left her mother.

"Growing up, I remember that my mother was extremely bitter about what had happened between her and my father. On the one hand she would urge my sister and me to respect my father, but she complained constantly about him, about their marriage, about what he wasn't doing now that they were divorced. She was most upset, I think, because she had worked to help put my father through college, and shortly after he got his degree he left her for another woman. My mother was a woman of some education who felt embarrassed to live in the working-class neighborhood we lived in. Nearly everyone else in our neighborhood was blue collar, working class; nice people, but my mother felt superior to them and she felt that we were being punished by having to live there, when if my father had stayed we'd be able to live in a middle-class community, the kind she thought as a schoolteacher she deserved. The financial hardship was a real burden for my mother, and she never let us forget how hard she had to work to make up for my father's absence.

"After my father remarried he moved out to Illinois, and when I was little, once a year, usually around my sister's birthday, he'd come and spend maybe a week with us. I think the only happy memories I have of my father are those times. He'd live with us in the house, sleeping on the sofa, and play at being a father. Because my sister had known him in a way that I never had, she was closer to him.

"He'd come and play the 'proud papa' role, but as I got older it just seemed like such a sham to me. What seemed to me when I was a child something good, and a way to have my father in my life, turned into something I really hated as I got older. My mother was always struggling to get child support from him, yet his visits gave him the chance to feel like he was doing something, being something that for me he would never be.

"My mother's bitterness has shaped my concept of men and love and relationships. She complained so much about what we didn't have because of my father that I grew up feeling—and admit I still feel today—that the only purpose of a man is as a source of financial support. It really hurts me that my mother, a woman who worked hard to provide for my sister and me, and who was, unlike my father, always there for us, was hurt so deeply. She made a lot of sacrifices for us to get a good education, and told us over and over that we could depend on that more than any man. I internalized her pain and her anger. She never once during my childhood had a relationship with a man that was satisfying. In fact she pretty much avoided becoming involved with men at all, and devoted herself entirely to my sister and me.

"I used to try to talk to my father about how rejected and abandoned I felt by him, but when I expressed my anger he just didn't deal with it at all. I never felt accepted by him.

And I always wondered: if I couldn't get acceptance from him, who would ever give it to me? I can't even stand to have the most ordinary conversation with my father, because even that brings up all the bad memories.

"And I guess it doesn't help, in fact maybe it makes it worse, that my sister is much closer to him than me, that she forgives him for anything he does wrong, and tells me that I have to understand him and try to forgive. To me, every time she reaches out to him she's just setting herself up to be hurt.

"Now my relationships with men are pretty rocky, they come and go frequently. I was in an abusive relationship when I was in college, and I don't expect a lot out of men. In a way I'm preparing myself to be alone. I'm preparing myself to be just like my mother."

When we met, Eunice was loath to criticize her mother for the emotional burden she inflicted on her daughters because of her own unhealed wounds. As our conversation progressed, Eunice told me that, at this stage of her life, she felt it was more important to recognize the emotional work she needs to do to save and change her life, rather than blame her mother for not doing what may have been impossible for her: forgive a husband who had hurt her deeply.

While Eunice acknowledges that she has a long road of healing ahead, Patricia McCreary has, after years of despair and pain, made a peace with her father and her past. A freelance graphic artist and illustrator, Patricia's large apartment—in a formerly derelict section of Washington that is now being gentrified and is home to scores of young professionals—is filled with reprints of the bold images of Romare Bearden, Japanese silkscreens, and framed black and white photographs of jazz greats. On the day I was there, sunlight cascaded through the sheer curtains at the ceiling-high windows as the leaves of philodendrons and ferns that hung from the ceiling arched toward the explosion of radiance. Barefoot, dressed in loose drawstring pants and a T-shirt, her cornrowed hair tied in the back by a strip of tie-dyed fabric, Patricia struck me as the essence of a centered, harmonious soul. Only when we began to talk would I learn how high a price she had paid to be free. She showed me some of the book jackets she had designed and brewed a pot of tea before we began the interview, sharing, in a voice at once melodious and urgent, details of the projects she was working on.

The youngest of eight children, Patricia, like Eunice, was the one child who had no relationship with her father. Patricia's mother was two months pregnant with Patricia when she left her alcoholic, abusive husband. "My mother worked for the District government in a social welfare agency. She had gotten married very young but was extremely resilient at raising us and providing for us. I don't really think that she ever really healed from all the years of abuse at the hands of my father. There were some brutal, terrible things that happened between them, but she pushed the past aside and focused on caring for us. My mother showed her love for us by providing. She felt that it was important for her to be strong, above and beyond anything else, and she never allowed us to show our emotions. I remember, as a child, if I cried or acted like I'd been hurt by anything or anybody, she'd preach about what a waste of time crying was. We were raised to hide our emotions, almost to act like we didn't have any, I guess so we couldn't be hurt, and to get on with life.

"My father was a seasonal father. He came around at Christmas, Easter, the holidays. Each year we could expect to have a great Christmas, to see the circus and the Ice Capades when they came to town, and in the spring to visit the monuments downtown. But he didn't provide emotional support to us. He was a Jekyll/Hyde personality. When he was sober he was loving, kind, patient. When he was drunk he was a monster. He'd call our house under the influence, and curse my mother and anybody who picked up the phone. He'd call twenty, thirty times, and scream in the phone, if it was one of the kids, that we'd grow up to be nothing. He'd come to the house and bang on the door all night long. When he was drunk he harassed us nonstop.

"As a result, my father made me feel fear, and I think that fear impacted almost every part of my life. My mother told us that our father was sick, that he had an illness, and she never talked against my father directly but all her comments about men in general were negative. So when she said that men were good for nothing, I knew she was really talking about my dad, even though she didn't say it that way. Nearly all of our conversations about men, whether we were joking or serious, were negative. It's funny how it became a self-fulfilling prophecy for my mother. My brothers were very unreliable, and often when she'd ask they simply refused to make repairs on the house we lived in. Yet my mom really catered to my brothers, she treated them like royalty, waiting on them, serving them, demanding more of the girls—and when the boys didn't pay her back with respect, I guess it proved what she believed. Men have therefore always been a kind of mystery to me.

"My perception of men was based on fantasy and rejection. My father broke all his promises, so I never wanted men to make promises to me. I had never seen marriage played out in our house in any positive or healthy way, so I developed very idealistic views about marriage, mostly from watching television. As I grew older, and especially by the time I was in college, I felt that if I could offer sex to men, I could cement their loyalty. All my relationships with men were based on sex. And often I drank to get in the frame of mind to have these relationships, to numb myself to what I was doing. I was promiscuous, did a lot of drinking, and was in a lot of pain all the time. Then I got pregnant by a guy I'd been involved with for three years, and we had a terrible fight and broke up. I had an abortion and felt like I was at the end of my rope. I remember one night I was in my room, and I prayed to God to just end my life if this was all the life I would ever have. It was an incredible moment. I cried out literally for God's help, and I felt at that moment God's presence. I joined the church and began the process of healing.

"Slowly I began to feel better about myself and my life, and about five years after my conversion I reached out to my father. On Father's Day I called my father and asked him to go to church with me, and told him that I would take him to dinner afterward. I had always felt inadequate and unaccepted. I blamed my father for everything. For example, I never held a job for a long time, which is why, I guess, I decided to freelance. I was famous for starting things and never finishing them. When I was a kid and I was involved in things at school, sports or plays, my mother could never come because she was always working, and my father just didn't. I remember looking into the crowd to see if my parents were there, and when I couldn't find them, feeling that whatever I was doing wasn't worth it because, I guess, I was doing it in a way to get love from them.

"My father was now sober all the time, and over dinner that day I asked him to forgive me for all the anger I had felt toward him, for blaming him for everything bad that happened in my life. Ironically, my father had a very hard time forgiving himself for what he had done to us over the years. Shortly afterward I arranged for him to come over to my mother's house and make some repairs on it—the plumbing, the roof, paint—with my three brothers. We were all kind of excited about it, my brothers and even my mother were looking forward to it. But the night before he was to do the job, my father got drunk. He hadn't had a drink in years, but he was so afraid of facing us that he started drinking. When I found out what he had done I told him that I still loved him, to sleep it off and come over the next day, and he did.

"He and my brothers fixed up the house, and pretty soon he and my mother began trying to repair their relationship as well. They had never divorced, and eventually my father moved back in. But forgiveness is a funny thing, how long it really takes. I was engaged to get married a while back, and a week before the wedding my fiancée broke it off. One of the reasons he broke it off, he told me, was that I still hadn't reconciled with my father. And he was right. I had forgiven my father with words but not in my heart. I'd still say and do things that showed that I really didn't trust him, and that I was still waiting for him to hurt me again. I was devastated and spent the summer meditating, praying, and trying to heal. I still had a long way to go, and now I was ready to do the real work that had to be done.

"My parents still have a long way to go. They live together, but I see some of the same old negative patterns emerging. It's like my mother let my father come back home so that she could punish him. Nothing he does is right, or good enough. She complains about him all the time. And it's like my father stays because maybe he feels like he deserves the abuse after all he put her through. I've talked to them both about getting some counseling. I can only hope that one day they will."

∞

THE MOTHERS OF both of these women were skillful and quite capable at meeting the *material* needs of their children against considerable odds. They kept food on the table, provided shelter, and even helped make it possible for their children to receive college educations. But they needed and longed for—and denied themselves—understanding, tenderness, the love of a good man, and the right to own and express and get beyond the anger they felt. In neglecting THEIR *emotional* needs, they neglected, as well, the emotional needs of their children.

Patricia's narrative is inspiring and satisfying because she grew into a woman able to do what her mother could not. She became the classic child who teaches the parents, the woman who learned to parent herself. In the same manner in which Michael Lindsey builds bridges to his father, thereby completing himself, Patricia's determination to love and accept herself inevitably affected her parents.

While a meaningful relationship with their ex-husbands was probably not possible for either Eunice or Patricia's mother, there were healthier alternatives to the responses they chose. The relentless criticism of the absent father was like a bomb that exploded not in the face of its intended victim but in the hands of the child the mother loved. The seeds of mistrust alienate children from their fathers (as some mothers may wish), but mistrust also alienates children from their mothers, and ultimately from themselves. Both Patricia and Eunice longed to love themselves and others. But having witnessed the bitter war of attrition waged by their parents, it was impossible for them to do so. While the actions of both fathers were crucial in impairing these young women, the mothers—as primary custodian of their children's souls (in most cases)—only exacerbated the problem by failing to forgive the fathers. Their good intentions were undercut by unresolved anger.

When Patricia's mother denied her children the right to express their emotional anguish, or to deal with and address the subsequent fallout, she established an atmosphere where the only safe place for such expression was underground, in secret. She terrorized her family with as much precision as did the violence of her former husband, and she did it through denial of the very real pain being inflicted upon herself and her children. Patricia's mother refused to allow her children ownership of the most natural emotions and the right to express them without fear or censure. Because she had denied healing and wholeness to herself, she could not offer it to her children.

The process of reunification of parents, whatever form it takes, moves the father from the margins of the child's life back to the center as a source of support, love, and counsel. Mothers then gain an active partner in the difficult ongoing process of child rearing. There will be disagreements, conflicts over values, over the interests of the child. These conflicts can be the springboard for creative solutions. Watching his parents compromise, figure out, and problem-solve teaches a child important lessons and skills about people and the nature of life, and confirms how much he matters to his parents.

THE MOTHER WHO SHOWED HIM THE WAY

These narratives twist and spiral and turn and land in different places, but spring from questions common to them all. These women found their power embedded in tortured relationships, the grip of childhoods past but not forgotten, marriage, and divorce. They found an unexpected faith and unforeseen strength in the awesome, rewarding, joyful, frightening task of motherhood.

For Charlotte Carter, Claudia Booker, and Yolanda English, living in the trenches of single motherhood forged a creative consciousness that gave them strength. For Janet Franze and Michelle Bachteler, the challenge was to learn to parent and trust themselves as women independent of their role as mother, all as a prelude to becoming truly creative/conscious single mothers. For Eunice Ogletree and Patricia McCreary, understanding and forgiving their own mothers was the first necessary step to creating their own healthy identities.

A single mother's spiritual journey begins long before she gives birth to her child, and it never ends. Her relationship with her family, friends, lovers, community, all determine her sense of motherhood. The spiritual life that each of these women has created is a rhythmic, surprising, offbeat ensemble of beliefs that essentially springs from their willingness to love themselves, their children, and others; and to commit this act of love consciously and conscientiously.

It is important to acknowledge that these women took *systematic* steps to create the kinds of lives they wanted. These are mothers who adopted a plan of action for their lives. Because they knew all too well the hazards of an improvised life, these women approached motherhood with faith and foresight, with optimism and definite goals. In their minds, they carried a picture of what they wanted for themselves and their children with them every day, and saw each day as another opportunity to bring this picture to life. What these mothers did, and more important, what they did *right,* can be emulated in the lives of all single mothers, for theirs is a methodology that emphasizes courage and compassion, love and respect by the mother for herself, her children, and her community.

As mothers, these extraordinary women called upon internal and external resources that made the lives they created for themselves and their children lives that were valued and sacred.

THE POWER OF FAITH

Each of these women possessed a belief system that was spiritual, religious, or ethical, and that they applied consistently to themselves as women and as parents. The belief system was built brick by brick from the lessons learned through their relationship with others, through the requirements and rigors of their faith, and through their constant need to evolve into fuller, more complete people.

WE ARE FAMILY

None of these women as single mothers lived in isolation from community or biological or surrogate families. They reached out to churches, schools, women's groups, circles of friendship and support, and created a wide net of psychological safety for themselves and their children. They did not hesitate to redefine the meaning of family when necessary.

IF IT'S BROKE, FIX IT

Psychological or family counseling and mediation was sought through mental health facilities, or through counseling with ministers or trusted friends. The need to seek professional help for herself or her child was not seen by any of these women as a sign of failure, but as a recognition that her family was wrestling with issues she was not equipped to handle alone.

I BELIEVE I CAN FLY

Optimism—a profound ability to expect the best, and to believe in their ability to create the best for themselves and their children—characterized these women. They were progressive, ambitious, relentlessly sought to improve their lives, and they did. The optimist's hope and faith and eager expectation of good allowed them to make a miracle every day.

A FATHER'S LOVE

While aware of the pivotal role they played in their children's lives, these women facilitated healthy relationships between their children and their children's fathers. They encouraged their children's love of their father, and when possible, worked with the father to provide a model of parental cooperation.

LET IT BE

In time these women grew emotionally strong enough to release the traumas of their own pasts, and to move beyond the difficulties with the fathers of their children. They decided quite consciously to step into the future, and to bring their children with them.

SOON HE WILL legally be an adult—the young man who, as my child, made me who I am. He admires the on-court artistry of Michael Jordan, and the films of Gerard Depardieu. I find rap songs lying in odd places around the house on much-handled, wrinkled scraps of paper; rhymes written in his small tense script. He is one of my favorite people to talk to, because of his humor, the depth and surprise and clarity of his mind, not just because he is my son. Our conversations reconfigure the world for me. His demons are familiar: a sometimes volcanic temper, sloth, and indifference in the face of a multitude of talents he wonders how to use.

When I married his father, my son became inevitable. When I left his father, he became mine. I neither knew nor suspected how he would create me. I was his mother, his single mother, singular, and because of him, never alone. His requirements pushed me always past the grasp of doubt and the onslaught of fear, because there was no time and he would have none of these things. There was a home of our own to make, and even if home was, at first, in a building and on a street whose best days were history, it still had to be transformed into home. And so it was, not only with plants and cheap but colorful carpets, but with scores of books filled with stories and words that would be the last thing he heard before sleep except "I love you."

Rebounding from a separation and divorce, building a new life from scratch, there were new perfect Stride Rites to buy for still-forming three-year-old feet. I, who in my pre-single-mother single woman's incarnation had shopped at Macy's and Bloomingdale's, bought my clothes second-hand, thumbing through racks of out-of-fashion, too worn, wrong color, not-my-size apparel—the scent of prior ownership still lingering in the fabric—for a thrift-shop treasure I could wear with enough style so that no one would know. This was sacrifice but I called it motherhood. To get us off of that street, where too many cars screeched by heedless of speed limits or toddlers at play, I taught part-time to supplement the full-time teaching. Five courses per semester, bussing across Boston, from black Roxbury to white Beacon Hill, hoping to impress the English Department at Emerson College and get lucky and get hired so we could move off the street that every day grew too small for a fast-growing boy. And even if it seemed that I never stopped grading papers or thinking about ideas for stories and essays and books to write, that was OK because my son needed the same things I did, a street with more room and people with different dreams, an apartment that would be like the life I wanted for him, one he could grow into not merely inhabit. This was ambition and hard work. I called it motherhood.

I had to be everything but of course that was not enough. His need to glimpse and learn the contours of a man's life and psyche and touch inspired me to imagine men as friends and advisors, and to invite them into his life and mine. The rigorous, selfless love Michael required sanctioned that manner of concern in me for myself. In time, all that I tried to offer to my son I realized I could indeed give to myself.

These transformations may have taken place in my life without single motherhood. But for over a decade, I raised my son alone. In many ways, my son's gift to me was not merely his presence or the opportunity to love him, but the *life* that resulted from the fusion of all this. I know how hard and how terrible and how enlarging and rewarding a single mother's life is. I would do it again. For Michael and I were creating a life. We were a family. We were creating one another/making each other strong. Observed in public, we were merely mother and son. No one could see the necessary battles waged and won, the tenacious bonds of loyalty and affection, the width and breadth of our suffering and sorrow, and how we managed to overcome. Strangers might have felt pity for the fatherless child, not knowing he had created, through his demands and his love, the mother who could show him the way.

MARITA GOLDEN is the author of four novels, most recently *The Edge of Heaven* (Doubleday, 1997). She has also written *Saving Our Sons: Raising Black Children in a Turbulent World;* edited *Wild Women Don't Wear No Blues: Black Women Writers on Men, Love and Sex;* and coedited *Skin Deep: Black Women and White Women Write About Race*—all of which have been published by Doubleday. Executive Director of the Zora Neale Hurston/ Richard Wright Foundation, Marita Golden is also on the faculty of the M.F.A. Graduate Creative Writing Program at Virginia Commonwealth University in Richmond, Virginia, she lives in Mitchellville, Maryland, with her husband and son.